Gardeners'
World magazine

101 IDEAS FOR POTS

1 3 5 7 9 10 8 6 4 2

Published in 2007 by BBC Books,
an imprint of Ebury Publishing
A Random House Group Company

All the ideas contained in this book first appeared in *Gardeners' World Magazine*

The Random House Group Limited Reg. No. 954009

Addresses for companies within the Random House Group can be found at www.randomhouse.co.uk

A CIP catalogue record for this book is available from the British Library

The Random House Group Limited makes every effort to ensure that the papers used in our books are made from trees that have been legally sourced from well-managed and credibly certified forests. Our paper procurement policy can be found on www.randomhouse.co.uk

Colour Reproduction by Dot Gradations Ltd, UK
Printed and bound in Italy by LEGO Spa

ISBN: 9780563539261

Gardeners'
World magazine

101 IDEAS FOR POTS

FOOLPROOF RECIPES FOR YEAR-ROUND COLOUR

Editor
Ceri Thomas

BBC
BOOKS

Contents

Introduction

You can't get much more instant gardening, or more instant satisfaction, than planting up a pot. A quick trip to the garden centre will reveal a tempting array of plants at their peak that can be grouped together to stunning effect. And if you fancy a change a few weeks later, you can swap things around or add some extra ingredients, with little effort.

For this book, we at *Gardeners' World Magazine* have chosen 101 of our favourite container planting ideas to inspire you to try something new. We've divided them into the four seasons for ease of planning and planting, and for good measure we've also included a few more that will look good all year round or can contribute to the cooking pot.

The secrets of success with container displays are to use good compost, to always put some drainage material at the bottom of the pot, and to keep on top of watering. It's no more complicated than that! (However, if you're new to pots or want a little more advice, you'll find plenty of helpful tips over the page.)

So whether you're filling the patio with plants or just want some colour by your front door to welcome you home, you'll find plenty of ideas here to brighten your garden and lift your spirits, every day of the year.

Ceri Thomas
Gardeners' World Magazine

Container maintenance

Throughout this book we will show you our favourite easy-to-create containers and give you all the ingredients you need to make them yourself. However, there are a few little things you need to remember when planting in containers, rather than into your garden, so here you'll find a few of the basic 'rules'.

(Where certain plants have particular cultivation requirements, such as acid soil or well-drained compost, this information appears with the relevant pot.)

Choose the right-sized pot. Sounds obvious, but it's easy to underestimate how much or, more rarely, how little growth a plant will put on in one season. It is important to think about a plant's needs when choosing a pot (some might prefer to be pot-bound), and whether you will be able to fit in all the plants you require for a display and give them room to settle in. If you are planting a more permanent display to last more than one season, find out what the long-term size of the plant will be, or bear in mind that you might need to pot it on. If your pot needs to sit somewhere specific, make sure it fits the space!

Check containers for drainage. Unless you're planting a bog plant, all plants in pots require drainage to prevent their roots becoming waterlogged and being deprived of the oxygen they need to survive. So, make sure the pot you use has holes for drainage, and if not, make them yourself. And to make doubly sure plants are not waterlogged, keep them happy by placing an inch or so of gravel, stones or crocks from broken pots in the bottom of your pot.

Get the right compost for your plant. Most plants will be happy with a general multi-purpose compost, but for any trees or shrubs that will stay in their pots for more than a year, choose a loam-based compost, such as John Innes No.3. Check the label of your plant or seed packet and find out if they have any specific needs, such as lime-haters requiring ericaceous compost, succulents and cacti needing specialist compost, and alpines wanting the very free-draining soil produced by mixing horticultural grit into compost.

Plants in pots are higher maintenance than those in the garden, so think about ways you can keep them, and you, happy in the hotter days of summer. When preparing the compost for the pot, mix in some slow-release fertiliser, such as calcified seaweed or Osmocote, to reduce your feeding chores. Remember that some plants, such as vegetables or greedy feeders like clematis, might also have specific needs.

To reduce your watering chores in the heat of summer it is also worth including some water-retaining granules. If you are going away (and we're not subject to a hosepipe ban), it's worth investing in a timer to water your plants. Simply gather together your pots, attach the hose system to the tap, set the timer and put a dripper into each pot – then you need not worry about asking a favour of your neighbour!

Before planting up, give potted plants a good soak. If you are planting a mixed arrangement it's also a good idea to lay out the plants in their final positions before you remove them from their pots. First fill the container with compost to the level of the base of your largest pot then place the plants (still in their pots) in position. When you are happy with how the display looks, remove the plants from their pots and backfill around them with more compost. Firm the soil, but don't press it down too hard or you will deprive the plants' roots of the oxygen they need to thrive.

Finish the soil level a couple of centimetres below the top of the pot, to allow for watering.

So that's the basics to remember, but now it's time to read on, to be inspired and, above all, to get planting!

Spring beauty

Time to plant: any time of year

You will need:
1 x azalea
3 x campanula
25cm (10in) pot
ericaceous compost

Azaleas will grow happily in pots, so if your garden soil isn't acid you can still enjoy these plants. Just pop them into containers filled with ericaceous compost and they will feel right at home. Take your pick of flowers from varieties in almost any colour, from deep red and pink to orange, yellow or pure white. Some even have a wonderful, spicy scent which fills the air on a warm day. Do note that while some varieties of azalea retain their leaves all year round, others are deciduous and lose their leaves in autumn.

For added colour, surround your azalea with three equally-spaced trailing campanulas. Again, you're spoilt for choice with these plants as they have blooms in shades of purple, blue or white. Planted around the edge of the pot, they'll tumble over the top and keep flowering after the azalea has finished, ensuring the display looks good well into the summer. Cut plants back if they begin to look messy.

TIP
Azaleas don't like drought conditions, so water them even when not in flower. Use rain water if possible, as tap water often contains calcium – which these acid lovers hate. Water regularly with a solution of ericaceous plant food too.

Tropical punch Time to plant: autumn

You will need:
2 x heuchera
2 x Japanese rush
4 x viola
25cm (10in) pot

Take your pick from the wide selection of colourful heuchera that are available. They stay looking good all year and work as well in the garden as in a pot. Position it at the back of the container and remove any leaves that die back. Replace the plant if its centre begins to push upwards with age.

Grasses are well worth considering for some winter interest, as many are evergreen and have an interesting structure. Japanese rush (*Acorus gramineus* 'Ogon') is perfectly hardy and looks good all year round. Plant it out in the garden in a moist spot when you eventually dismantle the container.

Although they'll bloom on and off during winter, violas really come into their own in the spring. Plant them at the front of the container, beneath the heucheras and the rushes, and they'll continue to bloom until the pots are ready to be replanted with summer-flowering plants.

TIP
Continually remove the old flowers from violas as they fade, this stops them producing seed and keeps them blooming longer.

Spring sunshine

Time to plant: autumn

You will need:
2 x pansy
2 x thyme
3 x ivy
medium-sized
window box

The hardy winter-flowering varieties of pansy (*Viola*) are the best bet for both winter and spring containers as they're rarely without blooms – even when other plants are shivering in the cold. Remove the flowers as they fade and the plants will produce more blooms, instead of diverting energy into making seeds.

Like most herbs, thyme (*Thymus*) is well adapted to the dry conditions often found in containers. In this arrangement we've used a gold-leaved variety, called 'Archer's Gold', to reflect the colour theme.

Tough enough to cope with the extremes of spring weather, from cold days to warm ones, ivy is great for containers and there are lots of different varieties to choose from. Plant them close to the front of the container so they trail over the edge and so their foliage will act as a useful foil for the cheery flowers that rise above it.

TIP
Using a window box for this display means you can enjoy the flowers from inside the house too, and just lean out to pick a sprig of thyme when you need it.

Zesty windows

Time to plant: autumn

You will need:
4 x tulip
2 x primrose
2 x sage
1 x winter savory
2 x ivy
2 x thyme
2 x lonicera
1 x pine
large window box

Either plant tulip bulbs in autumn or buy plants that are just about to flower in spring and drop them into the display. The bulbs can be replanted for next year.

Much larger-flowered than their wild cousins, these specially bred primroses (*Primula*) create a splash of bright colour at this time of year.

We've used a golden-leaved variety of sage called *Salvia officinalis* 'Icterina' to fit in with the rest of the colour theme and another great herb for cooking, thyme.

With a flavour similar to sage and the thyme that also feature in this container, winter savory (*Satureja montana*) is as useful in cooking as it is in a display, and the plants produce attractive lavender flowers in summer.

The trailing stems of ivy spill out from either end of the window box. This golden-leaved variety echoes the yellows of other plants in this scheme.

Most commonly used as a hedging plant, this golden-leaved *Lonicera nitida* 'Baggesen's Gold' makes a colourful addition to a container while young.

TIP
Although not a vital ingredient, we've used a young pine seedling as an interesting focal point in the centre of this box. It can be planted out into the garden afterwards.

Rich tapestry

Time to plant: autumn

You will need:
1 x hair grass
2 x thyme
2 x euonymus
2 x pansy
2 x curry plant
2 x ivy
large window box

In spring, hair grass (*Deschampsia flexuosa*) planted in the middle of the box, brings soft wispy foliage to the display. Planted out in the garden afterwards, it will produce shimmering flowers that last all summer.

Golden-leaved varieties of thyme, such as the 'Aureus' planted here behind the hair grass, are perfect for colour-themed displays. They're also great for cooking and are just as tasty as green-leaved ones.

One of the best foliage plants for containers, euonymus (*Euonymus fortunei*) looks good all year round, so it can be moved from pot to pot through the seasons. Plant one each on either side of the hair grass, and choose from golden- or silver-leaved varieties.

Two red-flowered pansies add a rich splash of colour to this foliage scheme, but if you don't want red you can take your pick from the huge range of colours available. All varieties will bloom for months on end.

The silvery foliage of the handsome curry plant (*Helichrysum italicum* subsp. *serotinum*), not only looks good but also has a distinctive curry-like scent. Plant one at at either end of the box above trailing ivy.

TIP
Always plant containers generously, cramming in plenty of small plants to create instant impact. However, be prepared to remove some as they grow, to leave more room for the remaining ones.

Cool blues   Time to plant: autumn

You will need:
1 x cordyline
1 x ivy
1 x purple sage
1 x curry plant
2 x pansy
1 x primrose
1 x lonicera
large, deep pot

The spiky outline of the central cordyline transforms this container. The trailing stems of the ivy at the front of the pot contrast dramatically with the cordyline's rigid, upright shape.

A purple-leaved sage (*Salvia officinalis* 'Purpurascens') tucked beside the cordyline echoes the colour scheme of this container, but it's just as tasty as the ordinary kind and looks good all year round.

The silvery leaves of the curry plant (*Helichrysum italicum* subsp. *serotinum*), which balances the sage on the other side of the pot, have a distinctive curry-like scent.

Pale blue pansies add colour and surround the cordyline. They'll rarely be without a bloom until the end of the season.

A world apart from the small-flowered wild form, a hybrid primrose is perfect nestled into the front of this spring container. Keep plants tidy by removing any yellowing leaves.

Young lonicera shrubs, such as this *Lonicera nitida* 'Baggesen's Gold', can be picked up cheaply from the garden centre and are perfect for pots while still small. Clip it regularly to maintain its compact shape and size.

TIP
This container includes some young shrubs which work well here when small, and will then get a new lease of life when planted out into your garden once the season is over.

Pretty primulas

Time to plant: autumn

Primulas are one of the most popular spring bedding plants, thanks to their cheery flowers, which come in rich colours. For the best plants, buy ones in individual pots, as these tend to have stronger rootballs than those grown in trays. Remove the flowers after they fade and take off any leaves that turn yellow.

As soon as they flower, you can see where this attractive species gets the common name of the drumstick primula (*Primula denticulata*). Take your pick from lilac- or white-flowered varieties. We've used both here and they sway above the flowerheads of the primulas.

Once you've finished with this display, all these primulas can be planted in a damp spot in the garden where they'll gradually spread over time.

TIP
Use equal numbers of the two types of primulas in this pot and echo or contrast the colours of the flowers, depending on the effect you want to create.

Fresh foliage

Time to plant: any time of year

You will need:
1 x hosta
1 x fern
1 x Japanese painted fern
1 x violet
large pot

Take your pick from the hundreds of colourful varieties of hosta available. After the plant's winter rest, the young, emerging leaves unfurl to reveal their brightest colours. Slugs and snails also find them very attractive, so be sure to protect them or you'll be left with leaves that look like doilies at the front of the display.

Any green fern will fit the bill here; sit it at the back of the pot and it will provide contrast for the colours of the other plants.

One of the most colourful ferns around, the Japanese painted fern, *Athyrium niponicum* 'Pictum', looks especially attractive when its fronds first unfurl in spring. Compare plants before buying, as some are more colourful than others.

Tuck it to the side of the pot with the plain green fern behind it to best highlight its foliage.

Violets bloom all spring long and are incredibly adaptable about where they'll live, enjoying sun or shade and really any type of soil. This variety, *Viola soraria* 'Freckles', has pretty white flowers which are covered in lavender-coloured spots. Over time it will spread to make a large clump, but it can easily be chopped back if it goes too far.

TIP
All these ferns will happily transfer into a shady spot in the garden once their work in the container is done.

Woodland wonder
Time to plant: spring

You will need:
2 x ranunculus
1 x viola
1 x spurge
1 x hosta
25cm (10in) pot

Ranunculus is one of the most voluptuous of all the spring bedding plants, thanks to its huge, silky blooms. It can be raised from seed, but if you buy plants, then wait until they're just about to flower so you can choose the best colours.

Their smaller blooms make violas a useful alternative to pansies if you want something more subtle at the front of your display. Available in an equally beautiful range of colours, many also have a wonderful scent that's worth bending down to enjoy. Either use plants or sow seed.

A classic woodland plant, spurge (*Euphorbia amygdaloides*) thrives in a semi-shaded spot where it will seed around to form large drifts. A young plant will be happy at the back of a container where its lime-green flowers will add height to spring displays.

Equally at home in a container or in a border, hostas are one of the most versatile foliage plants. Take your pick from the huge range of leaf colours, sizes and markings that are available. They perform from spring to autumn, returning each year after a winter's rest.

TIP
To get the best from this display, position it where it is protected from heavy rain and slugs and snails, this will prevent ranunculus flowers and hostas looking battered.

Daffodil delight

You will need:
10 x daffodil
1 x celandine
2 x corydalis
25cm (10in) pot

Years of breeding have created a huge range of different shapes and sizes of daffodil to choose from. Buy your bulbs in August or September for the best selection at the garden centre. Plant a group of 10 daffodil bulbs in autumn, in the centre of the pot, to ensure a bold clump of flowers develop.

The celandines we grow in our gardens are really only selections of the wild type that colonises damp areas of ground. There are some beautiful forms available, including double-flowered ones like this *Ranunculus ficaria,* and others with colourful leaves. Their dwarf sizes make them perfect for containers.

Another woodland plant that works well in a pot is *Corydalis flexuosa*. Look out for named varieties, such as 'Père David', as their flowers have the most intense colour. If you're moving the plant to the border after the pot is dismantled, position it next to something that performs in summer, as the ferny leaves of the corydalis naturally die down after the blooms fade, before returning in autumn.

We have popped in a few fir cones around the edge of the pot to fill gaps and add interest.

TIP
Dwarf varieties of daffodil look best in a pot display as they are in proportion to it. Once they have flowered they can be planted out in the garden or potted up and kept to one side for next year's container.

Tulip time
Time to plant: autumn

You will need:
10 x early-flowering tulip
10 x late-flowering tulip
5 x viola
30cm (12in) pot

A visit to the garden centre in early autumn will reveal an Aladdin's cave of spring bulbs. Choose from a huge range of colours, sizes and shapes of tulips, co-ordinating or contrasting them as suits your taste and display. It's best to plant tulips in late autumn, as this helps avoid the risk of a disease called tulip fire. Regularly water and feed tulips and, after their flowers fade, let their leaves die down naturally. Then you'll be able to move the bulbs to plant them again in autumn.

Not many plants can beat violas and pansies for their ability to flower all through the winter and into the spring. Position them around the edge of the pot to provide colour until the tulips bloom. The secret to continuous flowering is to remove the old blooms as soon as they fade to discourage the plant from wasting its energy making seeds. Most varieties have the added bonus of a sweet scent that fills the air on a warm day.

TIP
Use both early- and late-flowering varieties of tulip in the same container to keep the show going on longer.

Woodland gems

You will need:
1 x foamflower
1 x bleeding heart
1 x brunnera
wide, shallow pot

Easily mistaken for a heuchera, thanks to its attractive leaves, the foamflower or *Tiarella* tends to have larger blooms than its close cousin. There are many varieties available; all can be planted out into a moist, shady spot in the garden once the pot is dismantled, where they'll continue to look good all year round.

The common name of *Dicentra spectabilis*, the bleeding heart, is no surprise when you see the perfect heart shapes of its flowers. We've used the pure white form here, rising above the other plants at the back of the display, but you could use one of the equally attractive pink types.

The small blue flowers of brunnera look very similar to forget-me-nots, but this plant has the advantage of being a perennial, so it returns year after year. Look out for varieties such as 'Jack Frost' which have leaves with attractive silver markings instead of the plain green of the ordinary kind. In the garden it will grow in both dry and moist soils.

TIP
If planting in cooler weather, keep this pot in a sheltered spot, as the elegant foliage of the dicentra is vulnerable to damage from spring frosts.

School colours Time to plant: spring

You will need:
3 x ranunculus
3 x viola
medium-sized
window box

A showy cousin of the buttercups that grow in our lawns, ranunculus makes a spectacular spring bedding plant. We've chosen a bright orange one here, but you'll find plenty of other colours at the garden centre.

A colourful underplanting of violas sets off the ranunculus that sway above them. Take your pick from the rainbow of colours available. All will flower for months on end, going on until you're ready to dismantle the pot to make way for a new summer display. Either raise plants from seed or buy them from the garden centre.

TIP
Ranunculus flowers are a little delicate, so position your pot carefully and protect the plants from heavy rain. Remove them once they've gone over.

Cliff hanger

Time to plant: spring

You will need:
1 x thrift
1 x alpine phlox
1 x saxifrage
wall container

Found growing wild on sea cliffs and mountain sides, thrift (*Armeria maritima*) is a tough little plant with short, tufty foliage. It looks good placed centrally in this display where its bright pink flowers on long stems provide a focal point from late spring to summer. You'll also find a pretty white-flowered form on offer.

The low-growing alpine phloxes are a far cry from their towering cousins that grow in herbaceous borders. Equally as pretty, they are covered in blooms from late spring to early summer which tumble towards the front of the pot. Like the other plants in this container, they love a sunny spot. In this container we've used *Phlox douglasii* 'Lilac Cloud'.

Saxifrage provides dense cushions of green leaves from which brightly-coloured flowers shoot up in spring. Take your pick from the many colours available; this deep pink variety is *Saxifraga* 'Triumph'.

TIP
Alpine plants thrive in well-drained soil, so plant them in a pot filled with John Innes No. 2 compost with extra grit added.

Tawny terracotta
Time to plant: spring

You will need:
3 x *Verbascum*
'Helen Johnson'
3 x bronze fennels
3–5 sedums
5 x *Diascia barberae*
'Hopleys Apricot'
large terracotta pot

The coppery blooms of *Verbascum* 'Helen Johnson' take centre stage in this pot, the tall flower spikes rising above the other plants, giving height to the display. Don't be too quick to deadhead this plant at the end of the summer, as birds will feast on the seedheads and the spikes will look dramatic when outlined by frost.

To either side of the verbascum we have planted tall bronze fennel, whose wispy, feathery foliage adds texture and movement to the display. Cut this plant back to the soil each year, otherwise it could grow to 1.8m (6ft) high.

Softening the edge of the pot is low-growing purple sedum. We used two different varieties for added interest, *Sedum* 'Ruby Glow', for its green purple leaves and red flowers, and *S.* 'Vera Jameson', for its purple-pink leaves and pink flowers, but you can just use several plants of one variety if you prefer. Cut them back after flowering to maintain their compact shape.

The planting is finished off with the delicate flowers of *Diascia* 'Hopleys Apricot', which add spots of colour amongst the foliage and weave their way amongst the tumbling sedums.

TIP
Most of these plants are perennials and will keep on going year after year. However, diascias are short-lived, so they will need to be replaced anew each year.

Bold as brass
Planting time: spring

You will need:
1 x coleus
2 x dwarf dahlia
25cm (10in) pot

A plant more often confined to indoors, coleus has stunning foliage and is easily grown from seed. *Solenostemon* 'Kong Mosaic' is particularly striking, as it has huge leaves that are reminiscent of stained-glass windows. This plant will produce blue flowers, but picking off the flower buds as they appear will result in the plant producing larger, more impressive leaves.

You can count on dahlias to pack a colourful punch to any display, as well as providing a continuous supply of bright blooms. We've used *Dahlia* 'Redskin Mixed' here, whose reddish-purple foliage is a worthwhile bonus. Cut off faded flower stems regularly to encourage further buds. Other great performing dahlias for pots are the Gallery range.

TIP
Dig up the tubers of the dahlia in this pot and overwinter them in a frost-free place. Then you can replant them the following year.

Bright cube

Time to plant: spring

You will need:
1 x hosta
2 x busy Lizzie
2 x bugle
medium-sized, wide pot

Hostas come in a huge range of leaf shapes, sizes and colours and look wonderful underplanted with colourful foliage and flowers. To avoid leaves ending up like paper doilies, protect plants from slugs and snails. At the end of the summer, hostas can be moved into the border, where they will reappear each spring for years to come.

All busy Lizzies are happy in shady conditions. For the prettiest effects, look out for varieties with colourful leaves, such as *Impatiens* 'Fiesta Ole Peppermint' (shown here on the left of the pot).

Hardy and excellent for ground cover, bugles will weave their way under the other plants, quickly covering the exposed compost. At the end of the summer they can be planted out in the garden, where they will soon spread. This variety (to the right of the pot) is called *Ajuga* 'Golden Beauty', but you'll find a good range of alternatives at the garden centre.

TIP
Busy Lizzies are too tender to survive outdoors all year round, so take cuttings in summer and grow them indoors ready for planting the following spring.

Rose companions Time to plant: spring

You will need:
2 x miniature
patio roses
1 x rue
1 x pale
green thyme
3 x garlic chives
3 x small lavender
window box

Position two rose bushes at equal distances along the container. We used bright red roses, but choose your favourite colour. To keep the blooms coming, deadhead them as the flowers fade and apply a liquid feed every three weeks during the growing season. Roses often fall victim to pests such as aphid, but the other plants here have been carefully chosen to keep them at bay.

We planted the compact variety of rue, *Ruta graveolens* 'Jackman's Blue', between the roses to add texture and colour from its aromatic, intensely glaucous blue-green foliage. This plant is hardy, but if it should fail it is easily grown from seed sown outdoors in spring. (Beware of this plant's sap, however, which can burn your skin on contact.)

Thyme is known for its aromatic leaves and so is a good companion plant here (*see tip*). We used a variety with light green foliage, *Thymus pulegioides* 'Foxley'.

Garlic chives add height and movement to the arrangement, as well as more aromatic foliage to keep the pests at bay.

Lavender plants bring a silvery touch to the arrangement and a wonderfully evocative fragrance to a summer day.

TIP
Roses tend to be plagued by aphid, which are deterred by strong scents. The fragrant plants in this display will keep them at bay, but you can use any combination of strongly scented herbs, or other plants, to achieve the same results.

Rich red velvet

Time to plant: spring

You will need:
4 x dark Regal pelargoniums
4–6 *Trifolium repens* 'Dragon's Blood'
3 x *Alonsoa meridionnalis* 'Fireball'
3 x *Zaluzianskya ovata*
large terracotta bowl

The deep crimson petals of *Pelargonium grandiflorum* 'Chocolate' gives this display the rich red velvet of its title. There are many Regal pelargoniums available in this shade of red, including the popular 'Lord Bute', which would work well with pink, rather than orange, accent planting. Keep the flowers coming all summer by regular deadheading and, as these plants can be frost tender, boost your stock by taking softwood cuttings in spring or late summer.

The splashes of burgundy on the leaves of *Trifolium repens* 'Dragon's Blood' echo the dark Regal pelargoniums. This plant will spread happily to fill the pot by the end of the summer, so trim it to keep it under control, but let it go later if you want it to self-seed for next year.

Alonsoa meridionnalis
'Fireball' shoots up from the planting like sparks from a bonfire, adding dramatic spurts of colour amongst the richer tones and foliage. A perennial most often grown as an annual, you can sow seed outdoors in late spring.

Zaluzianskya ovata placed around the edge of the bowl softens the rich colours. The delicate, pink-tinged daisy stars will spread and tumble over the sides as the summer progresses.

TIP
Deadhead the pelargoniums and trim the other plants, which can spread quite quickly once established, to keep them looking neat and to encourage them to bloom.

Heady climber Time to plant: spring

You will need:
1 x star jasmine
1 x verbena
1 x heuchera
2 x thyme
large, deep pot
plant support

The star jasmine, *Trachelospermum jasminoides*, is a stunning, sweet-scented climber which will add height to a display. Train the stems to a wigwam of cones or an ornamental plant support. It is too tender to be left outdoors all year round in many gardens, so growing it in a pot is a great solution, as you can simply bring it indoors when the weather turns cold. To keep it in shape, cut back any unruly growth in early spring.

Verbenas are useful as they scramble through other plants and also trail down the side of a pot. We've used a purple one here, but there is a wide range of other flower colours to choose from. Either raise seeds in spring or buy young plants from the garden centre.

Don't worry if you can't find *Heuchera* 'Silver Scrolls', as there are plenty of other beautiful varieties of heuchera available. Most come in shades of purple or bronze, but you'll also find ones with strong leaf markings like this one. They can all be planted in the garden afterwards, where they will thrive in sun or shade.

Rub the leaves of any thyme plant and you will release its delicious scent. This silver variegated form looks as good as it smells, and the leaves can be used in cooking, like any other thyme.

TIP
Throw in an extra thyme plant to beef up the fragrance of this pot. Take cuttings in summer, to make new plants, and root them in gritty compost.

Tropical colours Time to plant: spring

You will need:
1 x lantana
1 x fuchsia
1 x isotoma
large pot

Lantana is best known for its display of multicoloured blooms throughout the summer. The rough-textured foliage is also extremely aromatic, having a musky scent. Be careful if you have sensitive skin, though, as it can cause irritation. Cut plants back in spring if they begin to get too large.

Fuchsias such as 'Thalia' make an elegant alternative to their more colourful cousins; all have slim orange flowers that hang in delicate bunches at the end of the stems. Place it at the back of the display so it can rise above the other plants and be seen. Like most fuchsias, the plants are tender so it's best to take cuttings in summer to grow indoors over winter.

Sometimes known as solenopsis, isotoma offers an explosion of star-shaped blooms that set off the other two plants to perfection and mingle amongst them. Remove the flowers as they fade to encourage the plant to produce more. If you can't find isotoma, try blue trailing lobelia or fairy fan-flower for a similar, and equally effective, colour combination.

TIP
All these plants thrive in a sunny position, but they will last for several years if brought indoors over winter.

Sky-high blue

Time to plant: spring

You will need:

**2 x large
agapanthus**

**large, square
terracotta pot**

This container is proof that simple arrangements can produce dramatic results. Agapanthus throws up breathtaking sky blue flowers on long elegant stems all through the summer. These plants may appear to be the last word in glamour, but they are also reassuringly easy to grow.

Happiest in pots, agapanthus flower most prolifically when they are slightly pot-bound, so plant them up in a container which is smaller than you'd usually use for two plants. Position the pot in full sun, water regularly, but sparingly, and feed the plant fortnightly during the growing season with a high potash fertilizer, such as tomato food.

Agapanthus can die in very cold spells, so move the container to a sheltered spot and protect the crowns over winter with a mulch of straw or ash.

It can take a couple of years for agapanthus to establish themselves, but give them time and you will be rewarded for your care with abundant flowers.

TIP

There's no need to underplant the agapanthus here, for two reasons. The plants speak for themselves with their dense mane of strappy leaves and they also don't appreciate the competition for nutrients from other plants.

Rich purple

Time to plant: spring

With its bronze-flushed, glossy leaves, *Pittosporum tenuifolium* 'Tom Thumb' is one of the most attractive varieties of this evergreen shrub. Plant it at the back of the container, but as it is a dwarf variety, 'Tom Thumb' can be left for a while as it will only reach around 90cm (3ft) high.

The purple blooms of fairy fan-flower (*Scaevola*) trail down to cover the edge of the pot. The easiest way to reproduce this tender plant is to take cuttings in late spring or summer and grow them indoors during the colder months.

In a pot where foliage plays a strong role, lilac-pink trailing pelargoniums provide more welcome flowers. For blooms all summer, remove fading flowers and feed once a week with tomato food.

The spiky leaves of astelia add a dramatic backdrop to this display. This New Zealand native isn't very hardy in the UK, so bring it indoors for the winter. If you can't find astelia, go for a bronze-coloured grass, such as *Carex flagellifera*, instead.

Echoing the silver of the astelia, *Heuchera* 'Silver Scrolls' ties the display together. There are several similar-looking varieties if you can't find 'Silver Scrolls'. All can be planted out afterwards in a sunny or partially shaded spot.

TIP
Brighten up your patio and paint your pot with masonry paint to contrast the colours of your chosen plants.

Mauve and metallic
Time to plant: spring

You will need:

1 x large or
3 x small
*Convolvulus
cneorum*
2 x French
lavenders
1 x large or
3 x small *Erysimum
'Bowles' Mauve'*
3 x *Sutera* Abunda
White
faux lead planter

The centrepiece of this display is silver-leaved *Convolvulus cneorum*, which looks good even after its white, bell-shaped flowers fade and its silver leaves remain, gleaming in the sunlight. These plants are well suited to containers, not least because they don't appreciate cold, wet winters, and benefit from being moved under cover at this time.

Erysimum 'Bowles' Mauve' adds height at the back of the display, its delicate stems holding its tall mauve flowers high above the other planting. Trim the plant lightly after flowering to prevent it getting leggy and to encourage it to keep flowering. It is an evergreen perennial, but it can be propagated by softwood cuttings in spring or summer if you want more plants.

French lavender (*Lavandula stoechas*) echoes the purple colour theme of this container and balances the arrangement, placed on either side of the convolvulus. Their delicate scent makes this a fragrant delight on a summer's day.

The pot is finished off with trailing *Sutera* Abunda White, which cascades down, softening the hard edges of the faux lead planter.

TIP
All these plants thrive in sunny spots with very well drained soil. So position the container carefully and add extra grit to your compost to improve drainage.

Spikes and spears   Time to plant: spring

The silver and dark green colouring of the ivory thistle, *Ptilostemon diacantha*, sets the scene for the planting here. If you can't get hold of this variety, try another thistle, such as the sea holly, *Eryngium*. Protect your hands and arms from its spikes when planting up this pot, and position it away from passers by.

The pheasant's tail grass, *Anemanthele lessoniana*, brings a soft texture to this display. This evergreen grass has something for all seasons: its brownish-green leaves turn orange in late summer, purple-green flower spikes appear in autumn before winter coats it in glittering frost.

The sword-shaped, cream-striped leaves of *Sisyrinchium striatum* tumble through the planting, topped off with slender spikes of trumpet-shaped yellow flowers all summer. For more plants, divide this grass in early spring, or grow it from seed in spring or autumn.

Day lilies bring a wonderful splash of colour. They may only flower for a day or two, but one bloom swiftly follows another from late spring into summer. We used *Hemerocallis lilioasphodelus*, for its very fragrant yellow flowers, one of many colours available.

TIP
When using any metallic container like this, insulate the plants against extremes of temperature by lining it first with bubble wrap or polystrene to just below soil level, before planting.

Tropical heat

Time to plant: spring

You will need:
1 x bromeliad
1 x Indian shot plant
2 x New Guinea busy Lizzie
large square pot

Although usually grown indoors, many bromeliads (*Guzmania*) are suitable for use outdoors in summer. They come in a range of shapes and colours, forming rosettes of tough, waxy leaves. Most produce a stout central stem topped with clusters of showy bracts, so look good centrally placed in a pot.

Prized for their large, impressive, often colourfully variegated leaves, and their blowsy flowers in hot fiery shades, cannas, or Indian shot plants, are guaranteed to lend a tropical flavour to any planting scheme. Place them at the back of a display to add height.

Available in a variety of dramatic flower colours that are often coupled with variegated or coloured foliage, New Guinea busy Lizzies (*Impatiens*) are reliable and easy to grow in pots, indoors or out. Thriving in sun or shade, they will flower all summer long. We've underplanted the cannna and bromeliad with two vibrant colours to add zing to the scene.

TIP
Guzmanias and cannas are not completely hardy and need to be protected over winter in a frost-free place.

Leafy opulence

Time to plant: spring

You will need:
2 x pelargonium
1 x castor oil plant
3 x lily
1 x *Helichrysum petiolare*
very large pot

Two vigorous fancy-leaved pelargoniums form the backbone of the display. We've used 'Black Jubilee' and 'Pink Happy Thought' but you'll find a range of different varieties on sale in garden centres. All can be propagated by taking cuttings in summer to grow indoors over winter.

The large, hand-shaped leaves of a single castor oil plant add drama to the display. *Ricinus communis* 'Carmencita' is a particularly attractive variety, but any one will do. All can be easily raised from seed in spring. Keep moving the seedlings to larger pots as they grow, before planting out in late spring.

Fading ahead of the other plants, the lilies' presence at the back of the display is only temporary. The gorgeous scent of oriental varieties, such as 'Aubade', more than compensates for its brevity.

The silvery stems of *Helichrysum petiolare* trail around at will among the other plants and over the edges of the pot. If the plant starts to get too large, simply cut it back and it will soon re-sprout. There is also a golden-leaved form of this handsome foliage plant called 'Aureum'.

TIP
As the lilies die off before the other plants in this arrangement, sink them into the main pot in easily removable plastic pots, so you can whip them out of the display when they go over.

Pink haze

You will need:
2 x marguerite
1 x verbena
3 x nemesia
large square pot

A dwarf pale pink marguerite provides height and structure. We've used *Argyranthemum* 'Summit Pink', but any variety of this reliable plant will provide a first-class display. Take cuttings in summer to grow indoors over winter.

Available in a wide range of colours, including peach, red and purple, verbena is one of the most adaptable of all container plants. We've used *Verbena* 'Lanai Bright Pink', but you'll find many varieties on sale in garden centres as both seeds and plants.

The semi-trailing habit of nemesia helps to soften the edges of the planting. We used a variety called *Nemesia* 'Blue Lagoon'. But, again, you'll find plenty of alternatives on offer. All are free-flowering and put on a superb show all summer long.

TIP
This is a great container for a sunny spot. Feed with tomato food once a week to encourage lots of flowers.

Colour ways

You will need:
3 x sedge
2 x dichondra
1 x rhodochiton
large, deep
rectangular pot

Grasses make superb plants for containers, where their striking foliage is a great foil for other plants. The colour of this bronze sedge, *Carex comans* 'Bronze Form', sets off the recycled copper water tank beautifully and helps soften its straight edges. At the end of the summer the plants can be lifted and replanted in the garden in a sunny spot.

Perfect for softening the edges of the container, the trailing stems of *Dichondra* 'Silver Falls' tumble to the ground. If you can't find two dichondra, try the more widely available *Helichrysum petiolare* instead.

A climber is a useful way of balancing the height of a tall container like this one, and *Rhodochiton atrosanguineus* is a spectacular tender climber from Mexico. A simple wigwam of bamboo canes is perfect for supporting the plant's stems; alternatively, try supports like trellis or a metal obelisk. Rhodochiton can be raised from seed sown in early spring, or buy young plants from a garden centre.

TIP
The plants in this container like a sunny spot but aren't keen on excessive wet, so dress the surface of the compost with grit.

Rustic charm Time to plant: spring

You will need:
1 x begonia
1 x pelargonium
25cm (10in) pot

Begonias with colourful foliage, such as 'Midnight Magic', are most commonly seen as houseplants, but they also make great additions to summer containers as long as they're kept out of direct sun.

Often thought of just for their flowers, there are many pelargonium varieties with equally attractive foliage. This is 'Meadowside Midnight', which has beautiful green-edged, bronze leaves with jagged margins. It's also a great flowering variety that's rarely without its delicate orange blooms.

TIP
This simple planting scheme works best with a simple container. Here we used a wooden butter churn bought at a reclamation yard.

Summer long   Time to plant: spring

You will need:
1 x aster
2 x 'Million Bells'
2 x pelargonium
1 x heuchera
large pot

The cheerful daisy-like flowers of asters provide a constant backdrop to brighten up displays when other plants are starting to flag in late summer and early autumn. Look for a dwarf variety such as 'Alice Haslam' when choosing one for a container, as tall varieties can reach up to 1.5m (5ft) high.

While more correctly known as a calibrachoa, 'Million Bells' looks like a miniature petunia. The flowers measure just 2cm (¾in) across but make up for their smaller size by smothering the plant with colour for months on end. The variety used here is cherry-coloured, but there are lots of different ones to choose from.

A summer stalwart, pelargoniums flower their socks off as long as the faded blooms are removed. Choose from the hundreds of different varieties that exist. There are all sorts of different flower and leaf colours available. To make extra plants, take cuttings in summer to grow indoors over winter.

One of the most versatile foliage plants for containers and borders, heucheras retain their colourful leaves all year round. This is 'Ebony and Ivory', but you can take your pick from any of the great varieties that are now available.

TIP
All of these plants will happily transfer into the garden – just pop them into a sunny spot when the display is finished.

Molten moment

Time to plant: spring

You will need:
2 x black-eyed
Susan
5 x creeping zinnia
large pot

Most black-eyed Susans (*Thunbergia alata*) have orange-coloured flowers, but you can also find yellow varieties like this one. Trained up a wigwam of canes, the plants will soon smother their support in blooms. You can buy plants from the garden centre but they are also easy to raise from seed in spring.

Not seen as often as it should be, creeping zinnia (*Sanvitalia*) is worth looking out for in the garden centre. This variety is 'Little Sun', which tumbles over the front and sides of the pot, covering them with yellow daisies. It flowers non-stop from early summer until the first frosts of autumn.

TIP
Training the black-eyed Susan up canes is a great way of drawing the eye upwards and making a small space appear much bigger.

Oranges and lemons

Time to plant: spring

You will need:
2 x osteospermum
1 x helichrysum
1 x lantana
large pot

Best known for colours such as pink and purple, osteospermum also has varieties in citrus shades, such as 'Orange Symphony' and 'Lemon Symphony'. Whatever you choose, remove the faded flowers regularly to encourage the plant to produce more.

Foliage plants can be as vital as flowers in a stylish container display: they provide a splash of colour that remains constant throughout the summer, even when flowering plants have begun to fade. This *Helichrysum petiolare* 'Limelight' has soft, furry leaves and is a vigorous grower. Prune whenever necessary to prevent it from swamping the other plants.

Lantana camara is a tender shrub with fascinating flowers that change colour as they age, giving a beautiful multi-tonal effect. However, be careful when handling the plant if you have sensitive skin, as the aromatic foliage can cause irritation.

TIP
These plants bask in sunny positions. They are perfect for pots as they will cope better than most if you forget to water them occasionally.

Sizzling summer cocktail

Time to plant: spring

You will need:

2 x bidens
1 x osteospermum
1 x lantana
5 x California poppy
1 x portulaca
large pot

The trailing stems and bright yellow, star-shaped flowers of *Bidens ferulifolia* make it a great choice for both containers and hanging baskets. It is easy to raise from seed indoors in spring.

We've used a dark purple osteospermum, 'Malindi', at the centre of this display, but there are lots of similar varieties. All will flower throughout the summer, especially if the blooms are removed as they fade. Take cuttings in summer and over-winter indoors to insure against losing plants in cold weather.

Look for a yellow-flowered form of *Lantana camara* to complement the other colours in the container. Wear gloves when handling the plant if your skin is sensitive, as the aromatic foliage can cause irritation.

California poppies

(*Eschscholzia californica*) are short-lived annuals, but add a good number and they will fill out any gaps at the beginning of the summer. This is 'Thai Silk Lemon Bush', but there is a wide range of varieties available. Sow them in spring in fibre pots.

Easily raised from seed in spring, *Portulaca oleracea* is a fleshy-leaved annual that thrives in dry conditions, so it won't be stressed by erratic watering. It needs a sunny spot for the best display of its silky flowers.

TIP
Many of these plants can be raised from seed. Sow them into fibre pots and you can transplant them into the container without disturbing their roots.

Silver service

Time to plant: spring

You will need:
3 x osteospermum
3 x helichrysum
3 x verbena
large trough

A trio of creamy-coloured, spoon-petalled osteospermums provide an eye-catching backdrop to the display. This variety is called 'Nasinga Cream', but you'll find lots of suitable alternatives at the garden centre. Keep removing the flowers as they fade to encourage the plant to produce more.

At the front of the container is a tangled tumble of tiny silver *Helichrysum microphyllum* leaves. This handsome foliage plant withstands periods of dry and hot weather without missing a beat. If it outgrows its space, simply cut back the excess growth and it will soon re-sprout.

The blooms of the verbena stand out beautifully against the silver foliage of the helichrysum. This variety is 'Blue Cascade' and is one of many on offer at the garden centre. Either raise from seed in spring or buy young plants.

TIP
Adding shimmering hints to any sunny spot, this cool silver, cream and mauve colour scheme looks particularly good in a metal pot.

Sun lovers

Time to plant: spring

You will need:
1 x eucalyptus
1 x coleus
1 x salvia
1 x gazania
1 x pelargonium
large pot

Although it will happily grow into a large tree if left alone, *Eucalyptus gunnii* also makes a great shrub with colourful metal grey foliage. Place it at the back of your pot and prune it back to its base each spring to encourage it to produce vigorous young stems.

Now better known as solenostemon, coleus is very easy to grow as an outdoor container plant. This variety is *Solenostemon* 'Peter Wonder', but there's a huge range available, each offering bright, multi-coloured leaves.

With so much colourful foliage here, it's good to include a few gorgeous flowers. And they don't come much more striking than the intense blue of *Salvia patens*. These tender plants need to be brought indoors for winter or raised from seed each spring.

The grey, strap-like leaves of gazania tumbling over the front of this pot form a perfect foil for its brightly coloured, daisy-like flowers. It is easy to raise from seed sown indoors in early spring, or buy it as young plants.

Although primarily grown for their vibrant flowers, many pelargoniums also offer colourful and shapely leaves. Some are even scented, releasing pungent aromas such as lemon and mint when the foliage is gently rubbed.

TIP

Gazanias need full sun for their flowers to open completely, so put this container in a bright spot for best effect.

Summer greens · Time to plant: spring

You will need:
1 x pelargonium
1 x bidens
1 x coleus
2 x pansy
large square pot

Scented-leaved pelargoniums are valuable not only for their aromatic foliage but also for their good looks. Select a plant with colourful leaves and place it at the back of the pot to provide interest all season: cream-edged 'Annsbrook Beauty' smells of lemon, or you could try the aptly named, brown-centred 'Chocolate Peppermint'.

For a sprinkle of pretty yellow flowers all through the summer, bidens is hard to beat. Its scrambling habit means it will grow through the other plants, filling the spaces between the foliage. Plants are easy to raise from seed if you can't find them at the garden centre in spring.

With their stunning range of foliage colours, coleus (or solemostemon) provide a good contrast for other plants. Either buy them from the garden centre or sow them from seed in spring. Remove any flower buds that appear, as these don't look very attractive and will divert energy away from the leaves.

Pansies are commonly used in winter-flowering pots, but they also bloom well during summer. Take your pick from a range of colours and either buy young plants or sow from seed. To keep them blooming for longer, remove the flowers as soon as they begin to fade.

TIP
Trim the scented-leaved pelargoniums regularly to encourage new growth and keep them compact in this display.

Exotic beauty Time to plant: spring

You will need:
1 x coleus
1 x nemesia
2 x New Guinea
busy Lizzie
large pot

For a knock-out effect and a touch of the tropics on your patio, use *Solenostemon* 'Kong Scarlet' (coleus) in this pot, with its huge, colourful leaves. Keep indoors until the danger of frost has passed in May or June. As snails and slugs love to eat this plant, stick copper tape or a smear of petroleum jelly around the top of the pot to stop them in their slimy tracks.

Although they've not been widely grown for long, nemesias really deserve to be popular, as they flower for ages. Many varieties have blooms that are sweetly scented. They mix brilliantly in this display, softening the dramatic foliage and flowers of the other plants.

Much bigger than ordinary busy Lizzies, New Guinea busy Lizzies (*Impatiens*) combine large, beautiful flowers with handsome foliage. They're great for a shady spot.

TIP
Keep this pot well watered as New Guinea busy Lizzies wilt fast when dry, but they will also recover quickly if given a long drink. Feeding with tomato food helps too.

Short and spiky

Time to plant: spring

You will need:
1 x ageratum
3 x pinks
3 x lilyturf
wide bowl or wide,
shallow container

Place an ageratum at the centre of this display, but look for a dwarf form such as 'Blue Danube' to match the compact size of the lilyturf and pinks. This is a tender bedding plant that can be thrown away at the end of the summer and bought fresh each year.

This container includes a variety of pinks called 'Mendlesham Minx', whose maroon and white flowers have a powerful scent. There are lots of other varieties to try, but not all of them are perfumed so be careful to check the label before you buy. Cut off the flowers as they fade to encourage more.

There are very few plants as black in colour as the lilyturf, *Ophiopogon planiscapus* 'Nigrescens'. Its spiky leaves make the perfect partner for the similarly shaped, silvery foliage of the pinks. When the pot is dismantled it can be planted in a partially shaded spot, where it will gradually spread and cover large areas of ground.

TIP
These plants won't cover the surface of the compost in one season, so make the container more attractive by dressing the soil surface with grit or coloured stones.

Seaside special Time to plant: spring

You will need:
1 x *Carex buchananii*
2 x blue fescue
2 x scabious
3 x thrift
recycled rubber tyre

Waving grasses pick up the seaside theme in this container. *Carex buchananii* is an evergreen sedge whose long orange-brown leaves arch above the other plants and looks good all year. This, and the blue fescue, *Festuca glauca*, are both excellent low-maintenance plants, requiring only minimal watering and a cut back in winter just before the spring growth appears.

The thrift (*Armeria maritima*) carries on the seaside theme and brings in splashes of colour with its profuse pink, white or purple flowers from late spring onwards. This plant still earns its place in late summer; the seedheads of the thrift turn papery yellow, so place the pot where the low afternoon sun will catch it and dramatically backlight it. Leave the seedheads for hungry winter birds and cut back the foliage in late February or March.

The lilac scabious echoes the purple accents in this pot. Here we used *Scabious* 'Butterfly Blue', which will flower from mid- to late summer. Keep deadheading it to encourage it to carry on blooming. If you want to keep this display going year after year, divide and replant this plant every three years to get the best from it.

TIP
All these plants thrive in very well drained soil and don't like wet roots. Plant them in a free-draining compost mixed with a few handfuls of horticultural grit or sand, and raise the pot off the ground with feet or large stones.

Hand decorated

Time to plant: spring

You will need:
1 x mealy sage
1 x ageratum
1 x cone flower
an old pot, approx
23cm (9in)

Blooming from summer to autumn, mealy sage is a reliable summer bedding plant. *Salvia farinacea* 'Strata' has blue and white flowers, but there are lots of alternatives to choose from. All are easy to raise by sowing seed indoors during spring.

The dwarf varieties of ageratum can look rather squat in a border, but at the front of a pot, as here, they are transformed. Ageratum can be found in shades of blue and purple, and can be sown from seed in spring. Once plants are blooming, it's worth nipping off the old flowers to encourage more buds.

The cheery daisies of the cone flower (*Rudbeckia*) never fail to brighten the mood. Look for a dwarf variety, such as 'Toto', and sow the seeds indoors during the spring. Like all of the plants in this pot it's an annual, so put it on the compost heap at the end of the season.

TIP
The simplest flower pot can be transformed with a dab of paint. For extra effect, scratch a simple pattern into the paint while wet.

French fancy Time to plant: spring

You will need:
1 x French lavender
2 x Swan River daisy
2 x helichrysum
23cm (9in) pot

French lavender, *Lavandula stoechas*, makes a pretty alternative to more traditional types of lavender. It flowers from late spring to summer with a wonderful fragrance. Put it in prime position in the pot and the silvery foliage will continue to look good after the flowers have gone.

Swan river daisy (*Brachyscome*) will tumble over the edges of the container and flower all summer. Pink and purple forms are a good alternative to the traditional blue-flowered varieties. Plants die in autumn but they are easy to raise by sowing seed indoors during the spring.

This gold-leaved *Helichrysum petiolare,* called 'Limelight', is a bright alternative to the more common silver-leaved version of this popular foliage plant. Although not considered hardy, it can stand mild winters outdoors if placed in a very sheltered spot. Trim back longer stems to spur on fresh new growth.

TIP
As the lavender plant is the focal point of this pot, cut back the blooms after flowering to keep it looking neat and bushy.

Bright and breezy
Time to plant: spring

You will need:
1 x ornamental grass
2 x pelargonium
1 x heuchera
3 x alyssum
25cm (10in) shallow pot

Grasses have become all the rage in recent years and many look wonderful in containers. *Hakonechloa macra* 'Aureola' is one of the finest, combining golden foliage with a billowy habit which sways above the other plants here. It will die back at the end of the year but will return in spring.

Pelargoniums are often ignored in favour of the many new types of patio plants, which is a real shame as they're such great performers and their flowers and leaves come in a wide range of different colours and shapes. It's best to buy plants or take cuttings, as they take a long time to raise from seed.

Good purple foliage is an important ingredient in the container gardener's palette and 'Black Beauty' is one of the darkest shades of heuchera available. It is quite a new variety though, so if you can't find it then try the more commonly available 'Silver Scrolls' or 'Chocolate Ruffles'.

Often thought of as old-fashioned, alyssum is still a worthy container plant. Low-growing plants like this lavender-coloured alyssum, or a lobelia, are useful as they froth over the sides of the pot and cover any bare compost with flowers.

TIP
Plant the alyssum around the edge of the pot and under the other plants and it will provide a lovely platform for them to erupt from.

Golden beauty

Time to plant: spring

You will need:
1 x conifer
4 x osteospermum
4 x ivy
large square pot

Not often used in pots, conifers make a useful centrepiece, as this *Chamaecyparis lawsoniana* 'Pygmaea Argentea' proves. It has bright, feathery foliage and a compact habit. It is also hardy and relatively drought-resistant.

The friendly daisies of osteospermum need sun to open fully. To keep the display looking good, remove the old flowers as they fade. If you can't find a yellow osteospermum variety, keep the colour theme going by using the golden or apricot-coloured daisies of gazania or arctotis instead.

Ivies are one of the most practical of all container plants, as they're hardy, drought-tolerant and look great all year round. This ivy has gold-edged leaves, but there are also plain green and silver-edged varieties to choose from. Cut back any stems that start to look straggly.

TIP
To get the best from all the plants in this pot, position it in full sun. The osteospermum blooms will then open fully and the conifer will keep a better colour.

Mix and match

Time to plant: spring

You will need:
**4 x *Pelargonium*
'Vancouver
Centennial'**
1 x fuchsia
standard-sized
window box

The variegated bronze and brown foliage of this handsome pelargonium ('Vancouver Centennial') complements the earthy tones of the terracotta window box. The flowers are vivid but quite sparse, allowing the foliage to take centre stage. Like all pelargoniums, it loves a sunny spot. To create extra plants, take cuttings in summer and grow them indoors during the cold winter months.

With its rich orange-scarlet blooms, *Fuchsia* 'Thalia' makes the perfect match for the fiery flowers of the pelargonium and a striking focal point. Like the pelargonium, it's easy to create extra plants by taking cuttings. Feed with tomato food to encourage plants to keep blooming.

TIP
Selecting similar tones of both plants and container helps to integrate the display. It also avoids dizzying colour clashes, which can be overpowering in a small space.

Chocolate and cloves

Time to plant: spring

You will need:
1 x chocolate
cosmos
4 x pink
tall, but not too
wide, pot

A chocoholic's dream plant, the dark red flowers of the focal plant, chocolate cosmos (*Cosmos atrosanguineus*), really do smell like dark chocolate, and the plant is rarely without them from July to October. Chocolate cosmos does have a tender nature, though, so either bring plants indoors for the winter or take cuttings in summer that can be grown indoors until the following spring.

When choosing a variety of dianthus to grow, be sure to look for one that has retained the spicy clove-like scent that pinks were once famous for. Many modern varieties are sadly lacking in this, so it's worth taking the trouble. 'Gran's Favourite' or 'Starlight' are both good choices. Remove the flowers as they fade and give plants a light trim if they start to get straggly.

TIP

This container combines two wonderfully scented plants, so make sure you position it near a seating area so that you get the benefit.

Moody skies Time to plant: spring

You will need:
1 x heuchera
1 x nemesia
1 x verbena
1 x marguerite
1 x salvia
large, square,
faux lead pot

Best known for their colourful leaves, heucheras also produce attractive flowers in spring and summer. These may be small in size, but the plant more than compensates with the sheer number of blooms it produces.

A classic plant for containers, nemesia is covered in flowers from early summer right up until autumn.

This verbena is a beautiful shade of lavender, but you'll find a wide choice of other colours to choose from. Either buy plants from the garden centre in spring or raise your own from seed or cuttings.

Marguerite, also sold as *Argyranthemum*, is a tender perennial rarely seen without its cheery daisy-like flowers from the start of summer until the autumn frosts.

Take your pick from the wide number of varieties of salvia available, in colours such as pink, blue, purple and red. All enjoy a sunny spot and many have aromatic leaves.

TIP
Check the hardiness of your salvia, as some are tougher than others. Take cuttings of nemesia and marguerite and overwinter them indoors as both are too tender to stay outside all year round.

Candyfloss

Time to plant: spring

You will need:
1 x pelargonium
4 x nemesia
standard-sized
window box

A classic plant for containers and here used as a focal plant, pelargoniums keep on flowering no matter how sunny or dry it gets. Their flowers and leaves come in a huge range of colours, shapes and sizes, so pick a variety that takes your fancy.

The secret to keeping *Nemesia denticulata* covered in its lightly scented flowers for months on end is to remove the old blooms as soon as they fade. Plants reach around 30cm (1ft) tall and once established are surprisingly drought-tolerant. The two most widely available varieties are 'Confetti', which is pink, and 'Blue Confetti'.

TIP
Keep this window box well watered and regularly remove faded flowers for the best effect all summer long.

Summer skies

Time to plant: spring

You will need:
1 x arctotis
1 x 'Million Bells'
1 x lantana
1 x salvia
shallow, wide pot

Arctotis is a pretty daisy native to the dry stony areas of South Africa – which explains its ability to withstand periods of drought in a container. Watch out for greenfly, as they are sometimes a problem.

Once thought to be a type of petunia, 'Million Bells' has now been recognised as a different plant, known as calibrachoa. Plants can be bought from the garden centre in spring, as they are propagated from cuttings instead of seed. Avoid over-watering them, as this can cause the foliage to turn yellow.

The orange-flowered variety of lantana is the one most commonly seen, but it's worth keeping an eye out for other colours, such as this attractive shade of pale lemon. Plants bloom over a long period, from late spring to late autumn. Be careful when handling this plant if you are prone to allergies, as the leaves can irritate the skin.

Few flowers are as pure a shade of blue as this salvia. Choose from the deep blue of the species or the pale blue of *Salvia patens* 'Cambridge Blue'. Both make great plants for containers as they are too tender to stay outdoors all year round. It's easy to make new plants by either taking cuttings or sowing seed.

TIP

Choose a modern variety of arctotis for this pot, as these have been bred to keep their flowers open even when the weather is dull.

Spicy scents

Time to plant: spring

You will need:
1 x 'Million Bells'
2 x scented
pelargonium
18cm (7in) pot

The rich cherry-red flowers of 'Million Bells' stand out beautifully against the green of the surrounding foliage. Buy plants from the garden centre in spring and be careful not to overwater, as they dislike having wet roots.

A quick rub of their leaves reveals the delicious scent of these leafy pelargoniums. We've used 'Shottesham Pet', which smells of fruit and nuts, and Fragrans Group, which smells of nutmeg. However you'll find plenty of other varieties on offer, with scents ranging from lemon to rose.

TIP
Position this pot in a sunny spot to get the very best from both plants.

South African sun

Time to plant: spring

You will need:
1 x arctotis
1 x osteospermum
18cm (7in) pot

Found in dry, stony soils in South Africa, arctotis is perfectly designed to put up with the dry conditions that container-growing often brings. Always choose modern varieties (such as 'Kiss Gold' and 'Kontiki Mixed'), as these are less sensitive to light conditions than older ones: this means they are less likely to close their blooms in dull weather. Cuttings can be taken at any time of year to create new plants.

Native to grasslands, rocky mountains and forest edges in southern Africa, osteospermum have long been popular for their brightly coloured, daisy-like flowers.

TIP
Both plants are too tender to reliably stay outdoors all year round, so either take cuttings in summer or bring plants indoors before the arrival of the autumn frosts.

Pebble beach Time to plant: any time of year

You will need:
1 x alpine pink
2 x pratia
1 x gypsophila
small round pot
pebbles
chicken wire

The dwarf size of alpine pinks (such as this *Dianthus* 'Fusilier') perfectly suits the proportions of this container. They are available in a wide range of flower colours and make neat, cushion-like plants. Look out for dianthus varieties such as 'Pink Jewel', whose blooms have the traditional clove-like scent, lost to some modern types.

In contrast to the upright shape of the pink's flowers, pratia spreads to make a low-growing mat of rounded leaves and pale blue flowers. Left undisturbed it would grow to cover a large area, but in a container it can easily be chopped back when it starts to overgrow its assigned space.

A white-flowered *Gypsophila cerastiodes* will tumble over the edge of the container, softening its appearance.

TIP
Make these alpine plants feel at home. Dress up a plain plastic container by hiding it inside a wire frame filled with pebbles.

Avant garde

Time to plant: spring

You will need:
1 x arum lily
3 x hosta
3 x lilyturf
large round pot

A stunning focal point in this container, while not hardy enough to survive outdoors all year long, the tender types of arum lilies are perfectly suited to growing in summer containers. To create new plants in spring, simply split established clumps into smaller pieces, each with its own roots and leaves, in spring.

Mirroring the shape of the arum lily's leaves, the hosta works well next to its exotic partner. This is a plain blue-green variety, but you'll find lots of other colours on sale at the garden centre, including silver- and gold-edged types. All are susceptible to slug and snail damage, so be sure to protect plants.

Few plants are such a pure shade of black as the lilyturf (*Ophiopogon planiscapus* 'Nigrescens'). Its evergreen leaves look good all year and plants will gradually increase in size to make large clumps. After the pot is dismantled at the end of the summer, the lilyturf can either be re-used in a winter display or planted in a sunny or partially shaded spot in the garden.

TIP
Arum lilies, *Zantedeschia*, thrive in moist conditions, so be prepared to water this container frequently to keep it looking healthy.

Out of the jungle

Time to plant: spring

You will need:
1 x canna
1 x pineapple lily
1 x sedum
large square pot

Surprisingly tough for such a lush-looking plant, a canna can survive outdoors all year round as long as it is given some protection during winter. *Canna* 'Tropicanna' has wonderful stripy leaves, but there is a good selection of varieties to choose from. All have brightly coloured flowers to match their striking foliage.

A dramatic flower for late summer, pineapple lily (*Eucomis bicolor*) is easy to grow from bulbs planted in spring. It comes from South Africa, so it isn't hardy enough to survive outdoors all year round in the UK. Bring plants indoors before the first frosts in autumn and keep inside over winter.

Usually grown for its broccoli-like late-summer flowers, sedum also offers attractive fleshy foliage that looks good from when the plant emerges in spring until it dies down in autumn.

TIP
Dismantle this pot at the end of the season to protect the tender plants which need to come indoors over winter.

Sea shanty

Time to plant: spring

You will need:
3 x larkspur
3 x feather grass
3 x coreopsis
window box

This annual relative of the delphinium, the larkspur (*Consolida*) is easily raised from seed in spring. Shelter it from the wind, which would otherwise blow over its towering blooms. At the end of the summer, the plants can be put on the compost heap, though don't forget to save some seed for next year.

Ornamental grasses have become incredibly fashionable in the last few years and none more so than feather grass (*Stipa tenuissima*), loved for its wispy texture.

Another great plant that's simple to raise from seed is *Coreopsis* 'Mahogany Midget' – a stunning variety that's covered in dark red flowers in summer. Plants reach no more than 30cm (1ft) tall, making them ideal for containers. Like the other plants in this combination, it does best in a sunny spot.

TIP
To reflect the seaside-themed planting, decorate a window box with some paint and by gluing on shells or old rope with bathroom sealant.

Happy days

Time to plant: spring

You will need:
1 x salvia
1 x marguerite
1 x fairy fan-flower
large pot

You'll find plenty of blue varieties of salvia on offer at the garden centre. All types of this tender perennial thrive in a warm, sunny spot and will keep blooming until the autumn frosts arrive. New plants are easy to raise by either sowing seeds or taking cuttings.

Look out for a yellow-flowered variety of marguerite, such as *Argyranthemum* 'Jamaica Primrose' or 'Cornish Gold'. This tender perennial will be covered in its cheerful daisies from late spring until autumn, as long as you keep removing the old blooms as they fade.

Soften the edge of the container by allowing fairy fan-flower to tumble over the front. *Scaevola* is a tender perennial from Australia that will bloom all summer long. It is easy to keep going through the winter by taking cuttings, which can be grown indoors while the weather is cold.

TIP
Plant the salvia and marguerite in the centre of the pot to grow together, and pinch out the young tips of the marguerite to encourage it to be bushy.

Purple passion   Time to plant: spring

You will need:
1 x blue potato
bush
1 x angels'
trumpets
1 x purple heart
2 x helichrysum
2 x parrot's beak
large, rectangular
pot

If you look closely at the purple flowers of the blue potato bush, *Solanum rantonnettii,* you can spot their resemblance to those of its close cousin, the potato. We used the variety 'Royal Robe' as a centrepiece, which has fragrant blooms.

One sniff of its beautiful perfume and you'll know why this tender shrub is called angels' trumpets. Be careful when handling brugmansia, though, as all parts of the plant are toxic. Take your pick from the wide range of colours available.

While purple heart is normally grown as a houseplant, *Tradescantia pallida* 'Purpurea' is perfectly happy outdoors through the summer. Ideal for a container, for the best colour leaves it needs bright light and slightly cramped roots.

Silvery felt-like leaves that are irresistible to the touch make *Helichrysum petiolare* one of the most popular tumbling foliage plants for containers. Look out for the golden and variegated forms as well. It's easy to make more plants by taking cuttings.

Its trailing stems of silver-grey foliage and bright orange flowers make parrot's beak, or *Lotus berthelotii*, a great choice for planting at the front of a container to soften its outline. Take cuttings in summer to grow indoors over winter.

TIP
Many of these plants have traditionally been houseplants in Britain, so don't forget to tuck them up indoors before the autumn frosts.

Drama queen Time to plant: spring

You will need:
3 x parrot's beak
3 x trailing begonia
1 x melianthus
1 x banana
very large, deep pot

Don't scrimp on the parrot's beak (*Lotus berthelotii*) in this arrangement – it's an exotic-looking, trailing plant with silvery foliage and bright orange flowers that resemble lobster claws. It's easy to grow, but needs protection during the cold winter months. Take cuttings in summer to make new plants.

We've used equal numbers of red-flowered begonias as parrot's beak, to echo the red tones of the banana leaves. However, you'll find plenty of other colours on offer at the garden centre in spring. Plant the tubers in pots, hollow side uppermost. Then grow on in a greenhouse until you're ready to plant up the container.

Melianthus is one of the most striking of all foliage plants, thanks to its blue-green leaves with serrated edges. A quick sniff of the leaves will reveal a curious nutty smell, not unlike peanut butter. Protect plants in winter as they are on the tender side.

Increasingly popular in recent years, bananas are now widely available in garden centres, and many offer a surprising range. We've chosen one with red-infused leaves, but you'll also find beautiful green varieties of both *Musa* and *Ensete* to choose from. Protect from winter cold.

TIP
All these plants are on the tender side, so protect them over winter and move the container outside when all risk of frost is past.

Golden fire Time to plant: spring

You will need:
For the main pot:
1 x berberis
2 x sanvitalia
1 x bidens
1 x sedge
large, wide pot

For right-hand pot:
1 x sedge
medium pot

For left-hand pot:
1 x *Euonymus fortunei* 'Emerald 'n' Gold'
medium pot

The rigidly upright stems of *Berberis thunbergii* contrast strikingly with the softer shapes of the plants below. We've used 'Pow-wow', but there are lots of alternatives, including ones with purple, golden or variegated leaves. All turn spectacular colours in autumn.

Sanvitalia's perfect daisy-like flowers wander happily through the surrounding plants. Like the other plants in this container, it loves a bright spot, but is also surprisingly tough and will keep blooming until the first frosts.

Easy to raise from seed, bidens has bright yellow, star-shaped flowers that cover its trailing stems all summer long. Save the seeds to sow the following spring. If plants get too big for their position, simply cut them back to size.

One of the most striking of all the sedges, *Carex oshimensis* 'Evergold' has a broad cream stripe down the centre of each leaf. The dense clumps will gradually expand over the years and can be split to make new plants.

Flanked by single plantings of sedge (right) and evergreen euonymus, this trio of pots makes a striking feature all year round.

TIP
As evergreens, the sedge, euonymus and berberis will look good all year so can be left in their pots permanently. The summer-flowering plants can be replaced by yellow pansies for the winter and 'Tête-à-tête' daffodils for spring.

Simple and sweet   Time to plant: spring

You will need:
1 x *Fuchsia* 'Thalia'
1 x fairy fan-flower
tall, narrow pot

Fuchsia 'Thalia' is a more refined-looking fuchsia for those who've grown tired of the blowsy skirts of the ordinary kind. Its narrow, pencil-like, orange flowers contrast beautifully with its bronze-coloured foliage and are produced in abundance. Bring indoors before the first frosts hit in autumn.

An Australian native that's brilliant for pots, the fairy fan-flower (*Scaevola*) is covered in its fan-shaped flowers from spring until autumn. As a tender perennial, it's not hardy enough to stay outdoors all year round, so take cuttings in summer to grow indoors over winter. It's a vigorous plant, so cut it back if it gets unruly.

TIP
Use a tall pot for this display, so the fuchsia really seems to rise above the fan-flower and creates a stunning vertical accent for your patio display.

Ruby red

Time to plant: spring

You will need:
3 x trailing
pelargonium
1 x purple basil
tall, narrow pot

One of the easiest trailing plants for a sunny spot, pelargoniums come in a wide range of colours including red, white, pink and burgundy. Given protection during the cold winter months, plants will last for several years. Alternatively, they can be replaced each year by new plants raised from summer cuttings.

As tasty as its more commonly seen green cousin, purple basil makes a beautiful alternative that's equally at home in container displays as it is in the kitchen. Harvest the leaves as you need them.

TIP
To keep both these plants looking their best, position the pot in a sunny spot away from cold winds.

Burning up
Time to plant: spring

You will need:
3 x gazania
2 x sanvitalia
2 x lantana
large pot

The bright orange daisies of gazania lap up the sunshine. Either raise the plants from seed in spring or buy them from the garden centre.

Few plants are as easy to grow as sanvitalia, which will keep on producing its small, daisy-like flowers come rain or shine. Plants can be chopped back if they begin to get unruly, otherwise they need little maintenance as few pests and diseases seem to attack them.

Rings of flowers that darken in colour as they age cover the lantana, producing a multi-tonal effect. This handsome tender plant can be brought indoors for winter, otherwise take cuttings in summer. Wear gloves when handling it if you have sensitive skin as it can irritate.

TIP
This is a really hot pot that loves the sun. Position it in a sunny spot for some sensational colour.

Steely grey

Time to plant: spring

You will need:

2 x begonia

2 x plectranthus

tall, wide planter

While many begonias are grown for their flowers, there is also a group that have beautiful, richly-coloured leaves, such as *Begonia rex*. They can be brought indoors at the end of the summer to make attractive houseplants.

An interesting group of foliage plants that works well in summer containers is plectranthus. We've chosen the purple-leaved variety, 'Mona Lavender'. You also find variegated and silver-leaved types at the garden centre. Take cuttings in summer, as this plant is too tender to survive outdoors all year long.

TIP

This foliage-based planting scheme makes a sophisticated summer display. For best results, position the container in dappled shade.

Gothic fantasy   Time to plant: spring

You will need:
5 x viola
2 x cineraria
1 x Regal
pelargonium
metal or faux lead
window box

Almost jet-black in colour, violas such as 'Molly Sanderson' will bloom for months on end as long as the old flowers are removed as they fade. If you need them, it's easy to make extra plants by taking cuttings.

With striking filgree leaves in a silver colour, *Senecio cineraria* helps lighten this dark-coloured planting scheme. Senecio are easy to raise from seed in spring, otherwise buy ready-grown plants from the garden centre. Surprisingly hardy, they can be planted out in the garden afterwards.

Worth tracking down at the garden centre for their dark, silky flowers, the burgundy varieties of Regal pelargonium; include the popular 'Lord Bute'. Like other types of pelargonium, they prefer a sunny spot and are easy to raise from cuttings.

TIP
If the violas begin to look straggly, give them a quick haircut and they will soon bush up and begin to flower again.

Flowery meadows Time to plant: spring

You will need:
1 x cornflower
4 x catchfly
wide, but
shallow, container

While the blue-flowered form of cornflower (*Centaurea*) is the one most commonly seen, this burgundy variety, 'Black Ball', is worth looking out for and makes a spectacular focal point in this container. Once a common weed on farms, cornflowers are sadly rarely seen nowadays. The blooms appear from late spring until midsummer.

Sometimes sold under the name of viscaria, catchfly (*Silene*) is an easy-to-grow annual that works well in both containers and borders. Its pretty flowers come in pink, white, blue and red. Their petals have a special quality that makes them appear to glisten in the sunshine.

TIP
If you are keen on attracting wildlife into your garden, then this is an excellent container, as cornflower is beloved by both bees and butterflies.

Pretty in pink   Time to plant: spring/summer

1 x marguerite
1 x chrysanthemum
1 x osteospermum
large pot

Marguerites (*Argyranthemum*) bloom from late spring onwards, and there's rarely a moment when this plant is out of flower until the frosts arrive, provided you remove the old blooms as they fade.

There is a new form of chrysanthemum on the market, known as 'cushion mums', which flower in spring as well as the traditional autumn period. Plants bought in bud in spring will produce two performances in one year, giving you amazing value for money. They are hardy enough to stay outdoors all year and are naturally compact.

A pretty daisy from southern Africa, osteospermums are available in a wide range of colours. This plant will flower from late spring to autumn and can easily be propagated from cuttings taken in summer. These are best grown indoors over winter as an insurance policy against losing the parent plants to the cold.

TIP
Marguerites and osteospermums are tender plants, so if you want to guarantee their survival, take cuttings in summer to grow indoors during winter.

Royal blue

You will need:
1 x bugle
1 x gentian
1 x heather
wide, shallow bowl
or container
ericaceous compost

The bronze-red leaves of this bugle (*Ajuga*) provide interest throughout the year and are a subtle foil to the intense colouring of the gentian flowers. Bugle is a really useful evergreen groundcover plant which will spread rapidly, forming carpets of leaves studded with short spikes of usually blue flowers in spring.

Prized for their amazingly vivid blue flowers, gentians (*Gentiana*) are one of the most beautiful of all autumn plants. The double forms, such as 'Eugen's Allerbester', are especially stunning. They are also much easier to grow than you might think.

The combination of deep green, soft-to-the-touch foliage and short spires of tiny pure white flowers that last and last make this bud-blooming heather (*Calluna vulgaris*) another autumn winner. The winter kinds will grow in any soil but, in common with the gentian, summer- and autumn-flowering heathers require an acidic soil. To encourage bushy growth, trim off the flower stems once they have finished.

TIP
The gentians and some heathers both require an acidic soil, so plant up this container using ericaceous compost.

On fire! Time to plant: summer

You will need:
1 x barberry
1 x checkerberry
1 x chilli pepper
1 x chrysanthemum
1 x ornamental gourd (for decoration)
large pot

A more compact version of a familiar garden plant, *Berberis* 'Tiny Gold' has golden leaves that turn brilliant red and orange before they fall in autumn. Although happy in the garden, its small size means that it will be perfectly at home in a pot for its entire life and, like all barberries, it's easy to grow.

Checkerberries (*Gaultheria procumbens*) form carpets of small glossy green leaves which are usually red-tinted in autumn and winter. The white flowers are followed by clusters of large red berries that release a pungent smell when crushed.

Picking up the colour of the non-edible checkerberry, the fruits of this edible dwarf chilli turn from green to bright pillar-box red as they mature in late summer and autumn.

They can be left on the plant for ornamental effect or harvested as you need them for the kitchen.

There are few plants more showy than dwarf chrysanthemums, regardless of the time of year. Their starchy appearance is not to everyone's taste, but they are unrivalled for autumn flower power. Although perennial, they are seldom worth keeping from year to year so they are best put on the compost heap after flowering and replaced with fresh plants the following year.

TIP
As it flourishes in acidic conditions, to get the best from the checkerberry keep it in its own pot of ericaceous compost and sink this into the display.

Autumn froth   Time to plant: summer

You will need:
1 *Aster* 'Monte Cassino'
1 ornamental cabbage
1 *Sedum*
1 *Carex* 'Frosted Curls'
large pot

An easy-to-grow hardy perennial, *Aster* 'Monte Cassino' adds height at the back of the pot and produces masses of tiny, frothy, white blooms with yellow centres throughout September and October. After flowering, cut it back by half and plant it out in a sunny border.

Thanks to their colourful pink, white or purple centres and bold shapes, low-growing ornamental cabbages and kales are supremely effective at the front of an autumn container display, creating a strong contrast with softer, blowsier flowers. Although not really edible, they are as easy to grow from seed as ordinary cabbages, so make a note to sow a packet next summer.

Ice plants (*Sedum*) have many virtues, not least their irresistibility to butterflies and beneficial insects such as hoverflies and bees. Their glaucous, succulent foliage looks attractive towards the back of a pot, and in autumn their pinkish-red broccoli-like flower-heads will rise above the kale.

As grasses fade, they have bags of charm and interest. *Carex* 'Frosted Curls' is a first-rate choice, growing only 15–30cm (6–12in) high. Put it where it can gracefully cascade over the pot's sides.

TIP
Cut the aster and carex back to the ground in spring and they will shoot afresh for the autumn.

Silver service   Time to plant: autumn

You will need:
2 x miniature
cyclamen
3 x thyme
standard-sized
window box

Until recently, many people only thought of using cyclamen indoors, but the development of tougher varieties, such as 'Miracle Series', makes them a great choice for winter pots.

Growing thyme in a window box makes a very convenient herb garden, as you can lean out of the window and pick a few sprigs every time you need them. Look out for varieties of thyme with attractive leaves, such as 'Silver Posie' (shown here), which look as good as they taste.

TIP
The secret of success with this window box is to make sure plants don't get too wet, as this can cause them to rot off.

Festive mix Time to plant: autumn

You will need:
1 x skimmia
3 x miniature
cyclamen
1 x trailing ivy
1 x checkerberry
large pot
ericaceous compost

Although many skimmias are grown for their berries, evergreen *Skimmia japonica* 'Rubella' is prized for its large clusters of pinkish-red winter buds that open in spring to reveal white, star-shaped, sweetly scented blooms. Both the skimmia and the checkerberry are lime-hating evergreen shrubs, so plant them in ericaceous compost.

The modern, tougher varieties of cyclamen, such as 'Miracle Series', are invaluable for winter pots. Tuck a few of them among the evergreens and they should receive just enough shelter from wet weather to keep them going throughout the winter.

Ivy offers a huge range of leaf shapes, sizes and colours. This variety is called *Hedera helix* 'Little Diamond' and has cream-edged leaves on trailing stems which tumble over the edge of the container.

Checkerberry, *Gaultheria procumbens,* is a diminutive evergreen shrub that forms a carpet of small glossy leaves tinted with red in autumn and winter. White flowers are followed by clusters of large red berries. Both the foliage and berries smell strongly of wintergreen.

TIP
Place the skimmia at the back of the pot where its handsome, dark and glossy leaves will act as a backdrop for the other plants.

Spike and span

Time to plant: autumn

You will need:
1 x yucca
1 x euonymus
1 x skimmia
1 x gaultheria
1 x thyme
large pot
ericaceous compost

Valuable for its spiky architectural presence, *Yucca filamentosa* 'Bright Edge' is perfect as the focal point in this pot. A sun-loving evergreen, it provides height and a contrast in shape. Despite its exotic appearance, it is surprisingly hardy and easy to grow. Take care though, as each leaf ends in a sharp spine.

Among the toughest and most reliable of all dwarf evergreen shrubs, *Euonymus fortunei* 'Emerald Gaiety' forms a compact mound of small silver-edged leaves. Thriving in sun or shade, it will withstand heavy pruning.

Unlike many plants that sport berries, *Skimmia japonica* subsp. *reevesiana* produces masses without needing a partner to pollinate it. The white spring flowers and bright red autumn berries are shown off to perfection in front of the yucca.

Gaultheria are available in a variety of berry colours, from white through to red, but those of *Gaultheria mucronata* 'Mulberry Wine' change from pale pink to a deeper shade as they ripen.

Thymes are available in many forms, from low and carpeting to upright and bushy. They also vary greatly in leaf colour, from golden-yellow to blue-grey. The thyme used here is 'Silver Posie'.

TIP
Both skimmia and gaultheria must grow in lime-free compost, so use an ericaceous compost to plant up this pot.

Boxing Day Time to plant: autumn

You will need:
1 x box pyramid
1 x mattress vine
10 x red pansies
long tom pot
2 sets of LED
battery-operated
berry lights to
decorate (optional)

A box plant is for all year, not just for Christmas, but in this display it is given a seasonal dash of colour to become the perfect decorative touch to your front porch or patio. Prune the box (*Buxus sempervirens*) to tidy up any stray stems before planting it up, and keep trimming it now and again over the rest of the year to help it keep its shape.

Place the mattress vine (*Muehlenbeckia complexa*) behind the box pyramid and gently separate out its tendrils so that it will wrap around it and weave through the pansies like a Christmas wreath, then trail gently over the edge. It will grow slowly at first then gather pace after a year or two, when you will need to trim it to keep it in check. If you can't get mattress vine, a dark green ivy would look equally effective.

Surround the base of the box with the pansies, allowing them room to grow over the coming months. Deadhead the pansies regularly to keep the display going right into spring, when they can be replaced by dwarf daffodils such as 'Tête à tête', or even snowdrops or crocuses.

TIP
Water the container sparingly every week or so over winter, and don't let it get waterlogged. From spring until autumn, water at least once a week and feed fortnightly with tomato fertiliser.

Ice queen

Time to plant: autumn

You will need:
3 x pansy
3 x daisy
1 x sedge
1 x hebe
1 x heather
3 x ivy
large pot

The pale blue of the pansy's flowers contrasts beautifully with the icy whites of the other plants here. A number of different varieties have been bred to flower in winter; they all tend to go dormant during the coldest weather but bloom again once temperatures rise.

Not seen as often as some winter-flowering plants, this daisy (*Bellis*) performs well in containers. This white-flowered variety matches our theme, but there are lots of other colours available.

The wispy foliage of the sedge (*Carex*) at the back of the pot lightens the heavier outlines of the other plants. This evergreen grass looks good all year.

Hebes are usually grown for their flowers, but this one also has attractive cream and green foliage. There are several varieties available, and all will thrive in a pot. They can be planted in the garden afterwards in a sunny or partially shaded spot, protected from cold winds.

Blooming from late winter until early spring, heather (*Erica*) is tucked in front of the sedge to add colour and texture.

A classic choice for softening the edges of a container, there are hundreds of varieties of trailing ivy to choose from.

TIP
Plant up this pot in autumn and it will sparkle until spring. Just deadhead the daisies and trim the ivy to keep it under control and it will thrive.

Bronze glow
Time to plant: autumn

You will need:
1 x phormium
1 x skimmia
1 x heuchera
2 x ivy
4 x pansy
large pot

You'll be spoilt for choice when it comes to picking a variety of phormium as a focal point for this container. We've chosen a simple bronze-coloured one, but you may be tempted by another colour, such as the gorgeous 'Platt's Black'. Plants will thrive in a sunny spot in the garden afterwards.

Skimmia japonica subsp. reevesiana is a tough little shrub and a popular choice for winter containers as its red berries shine out on a dull day. These are followed in mid- to late spring by fragrant white flowers.

Another plant that is available in a wide range of varieties is heuchera. This is a simple bronze-coloured type, but you'll find others with beautiful silvery markings or ruffled leaves.

Trailing ivy leads the eye down the container as the stems tumble down. Plants can be moved from one container to another over time, eventually making large specimens.

Choose a variety of pansy that's been bred to flower in winter for this pot, then plant it in abundance to create a great display that will look good into the spring. Remove flowers as they fade to encourage more.

TIP
Pansies add a vital floral touch to this display. They might fall asleep in the coldest of weather, but for most of the winter you should have plenty of blooms to enjoy.

Lighten up

You will need:
2 x cineraria
6 x miniature cyclamen
4 x ivy
square container

This handsome, silver-leaved bedding plant, *Senecio cineraria* (sometimes sold as cineraria), provides a bit of sparkle. Either buy plants from the garden centre or raise your own by sowing seed in spring. Pinching out the main growing shoots will encourage plants to remain bushy and compact.

This bright-red mini-cyclamen provides a vivid contrast to the sea of silvery foliage, but keep these plants sheltered from winter wet, otherwise they'll rot. Mini-cyclamen are also often grown as houseplants, so some aren't tough enough to survive hard frosts. For this container, look for a variety that is specifically bred to be hardy.

Brightly variegated ivy really cheers up a grey winter's day. Plant it around the edge of the pot so the stems can trail down. It can be reused in other displays when the container is dismantled or planted to climb up a support in the garden.

TIP
Make sure your pot has plenty of drainage holes in the base to prevent the compost getting waterlogged in winter. This pot has built-in feet at its corners to improve drainage.

Cabbage patch

Time to plant: autumn

You will need:
3 x ornamental cabbage
1 x heather
3 x ivy
wide round pot

These colourful ornamental cabbages are edible but are usually grown for pots and borders instead of the plate. Take your pick from the many forms available, although these purple-pinks are among the most lovely in soft winter light. They should last for several months, and look lovely covered by frost.

Winter-flowering heathers add a bright splash of colour in the centre of this display. There are lots of varieties to choose from, offering a range of flower and foliage colours. Give plants a trim after flowering and plant them out in the garden when you dismantle the container.

Ivy makes a useful evergreen plant for both pots and hanging baskets. Dot the plants between the cabbages so they cascade over the side of the pot. Look for one of the silver- or gold-marked varieties for a bit of extra colour. If plants get straggly, simply trim them back and they'll soon regrow.

TIP
If you have time to plan ahead, raise ornamental cabbages from seed, but if not, you can buy plants and drop them in for instant effect.

Black and white

Time to plant: spring

You will need:
1 x dogwood
3 x snowdrop
3 x lilyturf
very large, tall pot

The brightly coloured dogwood (*Cornus*) stems are revealed as the leaves begin to fall in autumn. Here it takes centre stage, surrounded by snowdrops and lilyturfs. This variety has lime-green bark, but you'll also find red- and black-stemmed dogwoods. To encourage the brightest-coloured stems, cut all the shoots back to a few buds from the base in late winter.

One of the first flowers to bloom each year, snowdrops (*Galanthus*) are always a welcome sight. Unlike other bulbs, it's best not to plant them as dry bulbs in autumn but instead to lift plants when they're in growth, as they settle in far better that way. Once they form dense clumps, split them into individual bulbs and replant them.

Few plants are as perfectly black as lilyturf. *Ophiopogon planiscapus* 'Nigrescens' contrasts stunningly with the lighter colours of the dogwood and snowdrops in this display, but, as an evergreen, it looks good all year. It will gradually spread to cover the whole of the pot with its inky-coloured leaves.

TIP
This is an excellent permanent display, as it just gets better with time as the plants settle in. Combine a cornus with variegated leaves, such as *Cornus alba* 'Sibirica Variegata', with bedding plants or bulbs to add summer colour and year-round interest.

Winter fire

You will need:
1 x dogwood
1 x fern
1 x skimmia
large, tall pot

The brightly-coloured stems of dogwood add a fiery touch to an autumn garden and they continue to dominate the show until they return in spring. This *Cornus* 'Winter Beauty' is an orange-stemmed variety, but there are also red-, green- and black-stemmed dogwoods. All benefit from being cut back to a few buds from the base in late winter to encourage lots of new stems.

Choose an evergreen fern that will look good all winter. There are plenty of different varieties on offer and all can be planted in the border afterwards to continue the display. Most enjoy a shady, damp spot in the garden and appreciate a thick mulch of garden compost or well-rotted leaves to help retain moisture in the soil.

Bright red fruits that last for months on end makes *Skimmia japonica* subsp. *reevesiana* an excellent choice for a winter container, and the show continues into spring when it produces fragrant white flowers. Don't let it get too dry though, or the leaves will turn yellow. Grow skimmia in lime-free compost, or water regularly with ericaceous plant food to prevent leaves turning from deep green to pale yellow.

TIP
We've scattered some pine cones around the edge of the container to add a little texture and interest and to hide cold-looking compost.

Plum pudding

Time to plant: autumn

You will need:
1 x skimmia
1 x ivy
1 x heuchera
1 x euonymus
large pot

A compact form, *Skimmia japonica* 'Rubella' is grown for its evergreen habit and dark red flower buds, which cover the plant from autumn to winter. This skimmia takes pride of place in this display and in spring will justify its place by bursting into bloom with fragrant white flowers. Plants can be put in a shady spot in the garden afterwards, where they'll thrive in moist, but well-drained, lime-free soil.

Tough as old boots, ivy is great for softening the edges of containers with its trailing stems during any season of the year. There's a huge range of leaf colours, shapes and sizes to choose from. All are easy to increase in numbers by taking cuttings.

Take your pick from the many different varieties of heuchera that are on offer. We've chosen a rich purple-leaved one, as it works well with the colour of the skimmia's flower buds. As well as being suited to containers, heucheras also make great groundcover plants in the border, thriving in sun or light shade.

An easy foliage plant for use at any time of year, *Euonymus fortunei* comes in a range of silver- and golden-edged varieties. Here it balances out the ivy planted on the other side of the pot.

TIP
If you want to add a little more colour to this display, plant a few spring-flowering bulbs, such as dwarf daffodils, in front of the skimmia when assembling the container.

Winning rosettes

Time to plant: any time of year

You will need:
1 x aeonium
1 x houseleek
1 x echeveria
small window box

Aeonium is a succulent that lends height to the trough. Literally meaning black head, 'Zwartkop' has become a very popular variety in recent years for its leaves, which start green and colour up with age. In winter the display is best enjoyed in a cool room inside.

Unlike the other two succulents, houseleeks can stay outdoors all year round, although they don't like getting too wet, especially in winter. If you can't find *Sempervivum arachnoideum*, with its silvery cobwebbing, there are plenty of others to choose from. All are happy in pots, as they're very drought-tolerant.

A handsome plant, *Echeveria elegans* forms rosettes of sea-blue leaves that gradually spread to form low clumps. In spring, as an added bonus, they will often send up unusual-looking orange-pink flowers. There are lots of different types to choose from, ranging from dark bronze to greyish-white. This plant will also need to be brought indoors during the winter months.

TIP
Dress the surface of the soil with pebbles to improve drainage and to give the display a natural look.

The three graces

Time to plant: any time of year

You will need:
1 x feather grass
1 x sedge
3 x blue fescue
large pot

Soft and silky to the touch, *Stipa tenuissima* sways and billows gracefully in the gentlest breeze. In winter, the faded leaves and flower stems of this beautiful grass are straw-like in appearance. To make way for fresh growth, cut back the whole plant to soil level in late winter.

Producing a fountain of narrow bronzy-brown leaves, *Carex comans* is one of the most popular of all sedges and even looks stunning in winter. Its leaves are slightly rough to the touch, so it is not advisable to stroke them – tempting though it may be! Tidy up plants in spring or summer by cutting out the old leaves.

Blue fescue is a spiky, silvery-blue grass that resembles a blue porcupine. There are many different varieties available, but for the most reliable colouring, choose a named one, such as *Festuca glauca* 'Elijah Blue'. Being evergreen, it will keep its colouring through winter and any dead leaves can be pulled out as they appear.

TIP
Position this pot in full sun to keep these plants happiest, but they will also tolerate some light shade.

Colour contrasts
Time to plant: any time of year

You will need:
1 x miscanthus
1 x glaucous hair grass
3 x lilyturf
large, tall pot

Prized for its striking creamy white and green leaves, *Miscanthus sinensis* 'Variegatus' lends height to the display, rising majestically above its cohabitants. Cut back old stems in early spring to make way for new growth. This plant will get pretty big if left to its own devices, but it can be easily controlled by dividing and replanting it each spring.

The chief attraction of glaucous hair grass (*Koeleria glauca*) is its pretty blue-green leaves, which are soft to the touch. As a bonus, in late summer this compact, mound-forming grass produces feathery flower-spikes that fade to a straw colour as winter approaches. Pull out any dead leaves in spring.

Tough as old boots, lilyturf (*Ophiopogon planiscapus* 'Nigrescens') will grow almost anywhere and its dark, nearly black leaves are a great contrast to its tiny pale pinkish-white blooms in summer, or to any other light-coloured leaves or blooms growing nearby. The silver-variegated kind, *Ophiopogon planiscapus* 'Variegatus', is also worth tracking down.

TIP
Use a tall planter for this display and it will echo the height of the miscanthus.

Feeling flush

Time to plant: any time of year

You will need:
2 x aspidistra
5 x lilyturf
large, tall pot

The classic houseplant of Victorian times, the aspidistra is gaining in popularity again, thanks to its striking foliage which is at its best in partial shade. In a few sheltered spots it can be left outdoors all year round, but in most areas it's best to bring the container inside for the winter. Look out for the variegated form, which has white stripes on the leaves.

Its jet-black leaves make lilyturf (*Ophiopogon planiscapus* 'Nigrescens') wonderfully unusual. This low-growing grass is a great foliage plant for both containers and borders. Here it is used beneath the aspidistra and contrasts beautifully with the white of the cistern and helps soften its edges. If plants become overcrowded they can simply be lifted and split into smaller pieces.

TIP
For a quirky touch, we've used an old cistern as a planter here. Have a nose around some reclamation yards – they are a great source of unusual items that can add an individual touch to your garden.

Blaze of blue

Time to plant: any time of year

You will need:
1 x astelia
2 x lilyturf
2 x pansy
large pot

One of the most striking foliage plants around, an astelia takes centre stage here with its beautiful sliver, strap-like leaves. Its tender nature means that it should be given some protection against the worst of the winter cold. Plants will gradually increase in size to form a dense clump of arching leaves.

The silver leaves of the astelia provide an excellent backdrop to show off the inky blackness of the lilyturf (*Ophiopogon planiscapus* 'Nigrescens'). If allowed to, the latter will slowly spread to cover the whole pot.

Easy to buy at any time of year, pansies will flower well in both the colder and warmer months. Keep removing the flowers as they fade to encourage the plants to produce more. Once the plants have run out of steam, simply replace them with fresh ones.

TIP
If you haven't got a coloured pot, *Ophiopogon planiscapus* 'Nigrescens' also looks stunning when set against blue glass chips or light-coloured gravel scattered over the compost.

Lock, stock and barrel

Time to plant: any time of year

You will need:
1 x silver birch
3 x soft shield fern
3 x heuchera
large, wide pot or
wooden barrel
loam-based compost

A birch (*Betula utilis*) is an ideal focal point for a pot, with its beautiful bark and its delicate foliage, that also provides dappled shade. When buying a birch, you can opt for a younger plant whose bark will take a few years to become white, or a more mature specimen that will already have whitened bark, but this will be significantly more expensive.

Despite being a native of damp woodlands, the handsome soft shield fern (*Polystichum setiferum*) copes well with dry conditions, making it perfect for growing in a container. Being an evergreen, it looks good all year round and it combines beautifully with the evergreen leaves of the heuchera.

This container features *Heuchera* 'Greenfinch', dotted amongst the ferns, which has stunning silvery-green leaves. But there's a huge number of varieties of heuchera available. Colours include bronze, purple, green and gold. All will produce pretty flowers on long stalks in spring.

TIP
Fill the barrel with a loam-based compost, such as John Innes No. 3, to provide weight and stability as well as longer lasting nutrition than a lightweight, peat-based compost.

Metal magic

Time to plant: any time of year

You will need:
3 x bamboo
1 x red hook sedge
tall, black planter or
other modern-
looking pot

The bamboo *Fargesia rufa* has a wonderful broad leaf that contrasts beautifully with the narrow leaves of the sedge below. Like the sedge, this bamboo enjoys moist conditions, so be sure to water the container regularly. Place the pot in a sheltered spot to avoid cold winds damaging them.

The dark brown-bronze leaves of this red hook sedge (*Uncinia rubra*) form a tufty carpet below the bamboo. From autumn to spring, they become even more colourful.

TIP
Scatter large black pebbles on top of the compost – they not only look good but also help to keep the plants' roots cool and moist.

Sea breeze

Time to plant: any time of year

You will need:
2 x euphorbia
2 x blue fescue
small window box
or other small pot

An underrated evergreen, *Euphorbia myrsinites* is an ideal plant focal point for a container, thanks to its sprawling habit and bizarre pale green flowers. These blooms appear in spring and are followed by attractive seed-heads in summer. Like the blue fescue, it's very hardy and looks good all year round.

Grasses are real must-have plants and many are magnificent. Blue fescue, which makes an evergreen mound of spiky foliage, is perfect for a container. The foliage has a steely blue colour that is evocative of plants by the sea. Look out for *Festuca glauca* 'Elijah Blue', which is one of the best varieties.

TIP
Position this container in a hot, south-facing spot, as these plants love sun and will easily cope with drought.

City slicker

Time to plant: any time of year

You will need:
1 x scabious
2 x heucherella
window box

This dark-flowered scabious (*Scabiosa atropurpurea* 'Chile Black') looks fantastic taking centre stage and rising above a platform of dark foliage. The plant is a short-lived perennial, but it can be propagated by taking cuttings in early spring. If you can't find this scabious at the garden centre, try the more widely available chocolate cosmos (*Cosmos atrosanguineus*) as an alternative.

Heucheras and heucherellas are great for containers as they come in some wonderful foliage colours. Here we've used x *Heucherella* 'Burnished Bronze', which makes an attractive mound in each corner, but you could use a heuchera if you can't find a heucherella.

TIP

This display will look good in any container, but a dark-coloured window box teamed with this simple combination of dark-coloured plants is the height of sophistication.

Potted fibre optics
Time to plant: spring

You will need:
1 x *Dasylirion acrotrichum*
large metal pot
succulent or cactus compost

This is a spectacular container where less is most definitely more. The spiky *Dasylirion acrotrichum* creates a stunning visual effect without any need for additional planting. Rather like a natural fibre optic light, its bristling leaves are dramatically set off when light filters down it, especially when its delicate, fibrous ends are backlit by the sun.

Native to Texas and Mexico, *Dasylirion* thrives in sunshine and well-drained soil, but is surprisingly hardy over winter if it is placed in a sheltered spot. It isn't happy in very wet conditions, though, so don't overwater it and give it plenty of ventilation. If you can, raise the pot off the ground on feet in the winter to prevent its roots sitting in waterlogged soil.

TIP

A mulch of gravel or pebbles will keep the soil surface of this pot looking tidy, or you could use glass stones to increase its luminous effect.

Formal dressing

Time to plant: any time of year

You will need:
1 x myrtle
2 x campanula
small window box

Box is a smart plant for a container, but it's worth considering other options that can also be clipped into shape. Myrtle (*Myrtus communis* subsp. *tarentina*) is an excellent evergreen, faintly aromatic with lovely white flowers in spring. An evergreen azalea would also work well as an alternative. Cut the myrtle back in spring and give it a tidy up after flowering.

Campanula portenschlagiana surrounds the myrtle to create a sea of blue when it flowers from June to August. The mix of informality and structure in this container works well, as the campanula spills over the sides and creeps up the stiff outline of the myrtle. The campanula will spread vigorously, so cut back the stems to keep its size under control.

TIP
Myrtle is quite hardy when placed near a protective wall and given good drainage, but in really cold areas take the precaution of lining the box with bubble polythene to insulate it.

Turning Japanese

You will need:
1 x Japanese maple
4 x bugle
tall, square planter

This dissectum variety of *Acer palmatum* has beautiful filigree leaves, but it's just one of the fantastic range of leaf colours and shapes that are available. Japanese maples are surprisingly quick-growing, so a smaller-sized plant will be fine. Acers don't like to be baked by the sun, so position this pot in a sheltered spot.

A great low-growing plant, the colourful leaves of the bugle (*Ajuga*) will soon cover the compost. In spring and early summer it produces dark blue flowers. We've used a multi-coloured variety called 'Burgundy Glow'. You'll also find purple and variegated varieties on offer. Simply give plants a trim if they grow too large.

TIP
The secret to success with this pot is to use John Innes No. 3 compost, as it retains its structure and nutrients well, and to water regularly during spring and summer.

Bamboozled

Time to plant: any time of year

You will need:
1 x woolly thyme
2 x houseleek
Giant bamboo stems or tall, slender pots

A furry-leaved cousin of the common thyme that we use in cooking, *Thymus pseudolanguinosus* forms a thin carpet that spreads out to cover the compost and then trails down the sides of the container. Plants need a sunny spot and really enjoy the good drainage that these unusual pots supply. If the plant starts to look a little unkempt, give it a quick haircut.

Houseleeks, or *sempervivums,* are incredibly easy to grow in a sunny spot with good drainage. You'll find an amazing range of houseleeks in shades of green, red and purple; some are even covered in silky strands that look like spiders' webs.

TIP
Giant bamboo stems make unusual containers for some low-growing perennials. You'll find them on sale at most garden centres and you can then cut them to size.

Gold and bronze pot

Time to sow: spring

You will need:
4 x bronze-leaved lettuce
2 x dwarf sunflower
1 x black-eyed Susan
large pot

The lettuces form the backbone of this display; they are one of the best vegetables for growing with flowers, as their leaves are so colourful and attractive.

Dwarf sunflowers add height and colour to the back of the container. Sow in spring, putting two seeds to a pot and then removing the weakest seedling to make space for the other one to develop. Alternatively, buy plants ready to plant in early summer.

Trailing black-eyed Susan (*Thunbergia alata*) tumbles down the front of the pot. Sow seeds in early April in seed trays and place on a windowsill. Grow in a warm, light place until they are ready to be planted out, transfering them into individual pots when the seedlings are large enough to handle.

TIP
The lettuces can be easily harvested without ruining the display by cutting just a few leaves at a time, as you need them.

A colourful salad

Time to plant: spring

You will need:
2 x red-leaved lettuce
1 x dwarf tomato
3 x nasturtium
2 x dwarf runner bean
3 x morning glory
3 x spiral plant supports
large, wide pot

A couple of loose-leaf lettuces, such as 'Red Salad Bowl' add bulk to the centre of the pot. They can also be picked one leaf at a time so you won't be left with a gap in your display when you harvest. Other good red varieties include 'Lollo Rossa', 'Bijou' and 'Delicato'.

Tomatoes are easy to raise from seed in spring, but you can also cheat and buy a plant from the garden centre. Dwarf varieties, such as 'Tumbler', are perfect for this container as it can sit to one side of the lettuce without getting too large, while its crops of sweet-tasting fruit tumble over the edge.

Nasturtiums' leaves have a peppery taste and their flowers make a pretty addition to salads. Sow the large seeds in spring in individual pots and dot a few of

plants to one side of the display. Watch out for cabbage white caterpillars, which can descend on the plants en masse and eat all the leaves.

Dwarf beans, such as 'Hestia', work well in containers. Sow seeds in individual pots in spring and plant them out into the middle of the pot.

The only plant in the container that can't be eaten is blue-flowered morning glory, (*Ipomoea*) which adds an ornamental touch. Canary creeper or sweet peas make pretty alternatives.

TIP
Put plant supports in the middle of the pot and let the beans and morning glory scramble up, adding height to the display.

Sunny courgette pot

Time to plant: spring

You will need:
1 x feather grass
1 x golden courgette
6 x dwarf rudbeckia
wide pot

The wispy leaves of the feather grass (*Stipa tenuissima*) in the centre of this display are soft to the touch and a great stress reliever if stroked gently! This perennial gives height to the arrangement, and can be planted in the garden in a sunny spot later. Either buy plants or try sowing from seed in spring.

Sow golden-skinned courgettes, such as 'Golden Dawn III', in individual pots indoors during April or May. Courgette fruits are best picked when they have grown to 15–20cm (6–8in) in length. Harvest them regularly to encourage further fruiting.

Dwarf rudbeckias form the bulk of this container, so sow varieties such as 'Toto' from seed in spring, or buy them as young plants from garden centres in May. Once they are flowering, deadhead them regularly by snipping off the blooms that have faded, cutting back to a bud lower down the stem. This will make the plant produce more flowers.

TIP
During the growing season, give an occasional high-potash tomato feed to this container. All the plants will benefit but, more importantly, it will help boost the courgette crop.

Herbs and flowers

Time to plant: spring

You will need:
1 x bronze fennel
1 x dwarf lavender
1 x golden sage
5 x dwarf cornflower
5 x love-in-a-mist
large pot

The tall stems of fennel are topped by attractive yellow flowers late in summer, while its leaves add a distinctive aniseed flavour to fish and meat dishes. The dark foliage of bronze fennel, *Foeniculum vulgare* 'Purpureum', makes it a popular choice for ornamental displays.

Although not generally used in cooking, lavender is a popular herb thanks to its sweet-scented flowers and leaves which are great dried in pot-pourri. *Lavandula angustifolia* 'Hidcote' reaches a compact 60cm (2ft) tall. An alternative plant is variegated thyme 'Silver Posie'.

Best known in its plain green form, sage is also available in several varieties, such as this golden one, *Salvia officinalis* 'Icterina'. It tastes just as good and is useful in pork recipes.

The intense blue of cornflowers is hard to beat. Dwarf variety *Centaurea cyanus* 'Blue Ball' is perfect for pots as it grows to only 30cm (1ft) tall.

More commonly seen in the flower border, love-in-a-mist (*Nigella damascena* 'Miss Jekyll') also does well in a container. Pale blue flowers are followed by puffy seed-heads that can be dried for arrangements.

TIP
Sow the cornflower and nigella seeds in biodegradable fibre pots outdoors between late March and early May, and then plant them, pot and all, in the container when they've made bushy young plants.

Ruby trough

Time to plant: spring

You will need:
2 x Swiss chard
2 x nasturtium
3 x pratia
large window box
or stone trough

The stems of Swiss chard are particularly stunning with the sun highlighting them, and the leaves can be lightly boiled or steamed as a spinach substitute. We used a red-stemmed variety called 'Charlotte', but a colourful alternative is 'Bright Lights', which will produce yellow-, white-, orange- and pink-stemmed plants.

Nasturtium (*Tropaeolum*) leaves have a peppery taste and are ideal for salads. Their cheery flowers are also edible. They are easy to grow from seed sown singly in fibre pots. These pots don't need to be removed when planting as they'll gradually disintegrate, allowing the roots to grow through.

Although not edible, *Pratia pedunculata*, a carpeting perennial, will quickly cover any bare compost at the base of the other plants and supply a succession of jewel-like, dark blue blooms. Pratia plants are available from garden centres, but if you can't find them, substitute them for bugles with colourful leaves, or purple-flowered verbenas.

TIP
A stone trough is ideal for this display to give all the plants room to spread, but a large window box or any other large container will also work well.

A place in the sun   Time to plant: spring

You will need:
2 x purple sage
1 x bronze fennel
1 x thyme
medium-sized
window box

Double up on purple sage (*Salvia officinalis* 'Purpurascens') for this display, as it is a wonderful container plant; aromatic with grey-purple hues, it's also delicious in cooking. The leaves can either be used fresh or left to dry and then stored in airtight jars.

Even though it will outgrow the box in a couple of years, it's well worth including bronze fennel (*Foeniculum vulgare* 'Purpureum') for its beautiful smoky-coloured, fern-like foliage and yellow flowers. Place it in the middle of the container and it will provide a focal point and a sense of height to the arrangement. Plants have a habit of seeding around, so don't be surprised if it mysteriously appears elsewhere.

A low-growing thyme finishes off the display, sitting at the base of the fennel. Its aromatic leaves are great in cooking, especially in chicken dishes. Take your pick from the ordinary plain green form or any of the golden or silver-edged types. They're all equally delicious to eat.

TIP
Herbs often need sun and good drainage to flourish, especially sage, so add some extra grit to the compost before planting and position in a sunny spot.

Strawberries and cream
Time to plant: spring

You will need:
3 x alpine
strawberry
2 x fleabane
large wall pot

Far more delicate in size than the ordinary strawberry, the alpine type has an exquisite flavour all of its own. They can be raised from runners like ordinary strawberries or simply sown from seed in spring. Feed with tomato food to encourage good crops. It's worth using some slug control, too, as it's surprising how far they can travel, even up walls!

Often seen growing between the cracks in paving, fleabane is a pretty daisy covered in flowers all summer long. Similar in looks to the common lawn daisy, the pink-flushed white petals of *Erigeron karvinskianus* gradually deepen in colour to purple as they age, producing an attractive multi-coloured effect. Cut back the plants in autumn to keep them looking tidy.

TIP
Try growing alpine strawberries and fleabane in the cracks in a wall. This will look just as dramatic and also makes finding the fruit much easier than when plants are on the ground.

A stitch in thyme Time to plant: any time of year

You will need:
4 x thyme
small window box

It's surprising how many varieties of thyme there are available. While the common type is plain green, there are others whose leaves are attractively marked with gold, such as 'Bertram Anderson', cream, such as 'Silver Queen', or silver, such as 'Silver Posie'. All produce purple, pink or white flowers from late spring to early summer, and all have good flavour for cooking. Some are mat-forming while others are more bushy in habit.

Once thymes have flowered, vigorous plants can be cut back to restrict their size and keep them bushy. It's easy to create new plants by taking cuttings in summer and rooting them in gritty compost.

Thyme is a useful addition to a wildlife-friendly garden, as its summer flowers are very attractive to bees.

TIP
You can plant just a couple different thymes in this window box, or you can use a mixture of more varieties for a pretty patchwork effect.

Index

Picture credits

BBC Books, Random House and *Gardeners' World Magazine* would like to thank the following for providing photographs. While every effort has been made to trace and acknowledge all photographers, we would like to apologize should there be any errors or omissions.

Mark Bolton p63, p65, p71, p73, p75, p79, p81, p141, p165, p197, p199, p201, p203; Jonathan Buckley p15, p17, p19, p21; Torie Chugg p67, p69, p121, p123, p125, p127, p129, p131, p133, p135, p177; Paul Debois p23, p137; Caroline Hughes p1179, p181, p183; Stephen Marwood p11, p13, p49, p51, p55, p83, p85, p87, p91, p93, p95, p97, p99, p161, p163, p185, p187, p191, p207; Ben Murphy p39, p45, p47, p53, p57, p59, p89, p155, p189; Freia Turland/Dig Pictures p25, p27, p29, p31, p33, p35, p37, p41, p43, p61, p101, p105, p107, p109, p111, p113, p115, p117, p119, p139, p143, p145, p147, p149, p151, p153, p167, p169, p171, p173, p175, p193, p195, p205, p207, p209, p211; William Shaw p157, p159.

With thanks to: Ros Badger, Adam Caplin, Martin Fish, Elspeth Thompson, Paul Williams, Sarah Wilson.